To Dear Mike + Maureen
Merry Christmas in Aus
Lisa + Greg.

CATRIONA'S **AUSTRALIA**
MY FAVOURITE AUSSIE LOCATIONS

CATRIONA'S AUSTRALIA
MY FAVOURITE AUSSIE LOCATIONS

CATRIONA ROWNTREE

JAMIE DURIE PUBLISHING

PUBLISHED BY Jamie Durie Publishing
JPD MEDIA PTY LTD
ABN 83 098 894 761
35 Albany Street
Crows Nest NSW 2065
PHONE: + 61 2 9026 7444
FAX: + 61 2 9026 7475

FOUNDER AND EDITORIAL DIRECTOR: Jamie Durie
GROUP CREATIVE DIRECTOR: Nadine Bush

PUBLISHER: Nicola Hartley
DEVELOPMENTAL EDITOR: Bettina Hodgson
CREATIVE DIRECTOR: Amanda Emmerson
DESIGN AND ILLUSTRATION: Criena Court
PUBLISHING SERVICES MANAGER: Belinda Smithyman
PUBLISHING ASSISTANT: Michelle Kavanagh
EDITOR AND RESEARCHER: Joanne Holliman
COMMISSIONED PHOTOGRAPHY: Jason Busch

DISTRIBUTED BY: HarperCollinsPublishers Australia

© 2006 TEXT: Catriona Rowntree
© 2006 DESIGN AND COMMISSIONED PHOTOGRAPHY:
Jamie Durie Publishing

Rowntree, Catriona.
Catriona's Australia: my favourite Aussie locations.

Includes index.
ISBN 0 9757355 9 4.
1. Rowntree, Catriona. 2. Australia – Guidebooks. 3. Australia – Pictorial works.
I. Holliman, Joanne. II. Busch, Jason. III. Title.
919.407

Set in Gotham on InDesign
Printed in Singapore by Tien Wah Press
First printed in 2006

10 9 8 7 6 5 4 3 2 1

Thank you so much to my friends and family for sticking by me while I wrote this book. Your support, patience and love is just amazing. As is the entire team at JDP. I am full of gratitude for your professionalism, endless smiles and unwavering faith. Jamie Durie, thankyou for this opportunity, you are a complete inspiration to us all. My *Getaway* colleagues, I adore you. Finally, to all the people who alllowed me to include them in this book, thankyou and enjoy the compliment.

THE PUBLISHERS WOULD ALSO LIKE TO THANK
FOR ACCOMMODATION ASSISTANCE
Akuna House and Byron Beach Realty, Byron Bay, (02) 6685 6402; Avoca Beach Lighthouse and George Brand Real Estate, Avoca Beach; Beach Club Resort and Reef View Hotel, Hamilton Island; Hotel Lindrum, Melbourne; Peppers Convent, Pokolbin.

FOR LOCATION ASSISTANCE
BYRON BAY AND HINTERLAND: Akuna House, Gaia Retreat, The Beach Hotel.
CENTRAL COAST AND SURROUNDS: Glenworth Valley, Hawkesbury River Escapes, The Boat House on Hawkesbury, Phil Mason.
HAMILTON ISLAND: Beach Club Resort, Reef View Hotel, Fantasea Cruises, Sunsail.
HUNTER VALLEY: Peppers Convent, Roberts Restaurant, Peppertree Wines, Hunter Valley Gardens, Tyrrell's Wines, McGuigan's Wines, Terrace Valley Wines.
MELBOURNE: Hotel Lindrum, Melbourne Sports Tours, The Supper Club, Melbourne Rowing Club, Royal Botanic Gardens Melbourne.
SYDNEY: Manly Kayaks, Sydney BridgeClimb, Lord Nelson Hotel, Opera Bar.

FOR PROPS ASSISTANCE
Lee Mathews Workroom, Bow Wow, Village Living, Beachhouse Collections, Beach General, Ici Et La, Jets, Samsonite.

A very special thank you to Tourism Queensland, Tourism New South Wales, Tourism Victoria, Tourism Tasmania, South Australian Tourism Commision, Toursim Western Australia and everyone who supplied additional photography for this book.

ADDITIONAL PHOTOGRAPHY SUPPLIED COURTESY OF:
Pp 10–11: Barossa Wine and Visitor Information Centre; South Australian Tourism Commission, photography by Milton Wordley. P 13: Voyages Bedarra Island. Pp 14–15: Riverfestival Brisbane; Conrad Treasury, photography by www.vincentlong.com; Tourism Queensland, photography by Peter Lik. Pp 18–19: Canberra & Region Visitors Centre; Dawn Drifters; National Museum of Australia, photography by George Serras and Dean McNicoll; Questacon. P 20: King Leopold Air; Tourism Western Australia. Pp 22–23: Como Cottage Accommodation; Destination Yarra Valley Dandenong Ranges. Pp 24–25: Tourism Tasmania, photography by Steve Lovegrove. Pp 26–27: Hawkesbury River Escapes. Pp 28–29: Elise Pascoe International Cooking School; Tourism Woollongong. Pp 30–31: Skyfarm. Pp 32–33: King Island Tourist Inc, photography by Wendy Reed and Margaret Jones; Tourism Tasmania, photography by Nick Osborne and Chris Bell. Pp 34–35: Voyages Kings Canyon Resort. Pp 36–37: Tourism Tasmania, photography by Ray Joyce and John de la Roche. Pp 38–39: Capella Lodge. Pp 42–43: Eagle School of Microlighting; Villa Gusto; Mt Buffalo Chalet. P 44: Western Australian Tourism. P 46–47: The Boathouse; Tourism North Queensland. P 48–49: Tumbling Waters Retreat; Tourism Wollongong. P 52–53: Yarra Valley Visitor Information Centre; Healesville Hotel, photography by www.markchew.com.au; Healesville Sanctuary; Tourism Victoria. Pp 54–55: Young Visitor Information Centre. P 58–59: Bay of Fires Walk; Tourism Tasmania, photography by George Apostolidis. P 60–61: Lake House. Pp 62–63: The Original Eumundi Markets; Tourism Queensland, photography by Peter Lik. Pp 64–65: Burrawang West Station, photography by Michael Gebecki and Robert Koppes. Pp 66–67: French Island Llama Experience; McLeod Eco Farm; Tourism Victoria. Pp 70–71: Camp Eden Health Retreat; Conrad Jupiters; Tourism Queensland, photography by Peter Lik. P 73: Henry Jones Art Hotel; Fish Frenzy; Roger Palmer; Tourism Tasmania, photography by Richard Eastwood. Pp 74–75: Kangaroo Island Gateway Visitor Information Centre. Pp 76–77: J. Boag & Son Photo Library; Hatherley House; Tourism Tasmania, photography by J.P. and E. Baker, Chris McLennan and Owen Hughes. Pp 78–79: Maldon Lolly Shop; Maldon Tourist Authority, photography by Debbie Walkden. Pp 80–81: Moondance Lodge; Yallingup Surf School, photography by Twig; Leeuwin Estate, www.leeuwinestate.com.au; Vasse Felix. Pp 82–83: Tourism Victoria. Pp 84–85: Heronswood, photography by The Digger's Club; Winelounge; Mornington Peninsula Tourism and Visitor Information Centre. Pp 86–87: Mojosurf Australia. Pp 88–89: Borrodell on the Mount; Bloodwood Estate. Pp 90–91: Orion Expedition Cruises. Pp 92–93: Rundells Horse Riding; Tourism Victoria, photography by Peter Dunphy. Pp 94–95: Smoky Cape Lighthouse, photography by Stuart Poignand; Great Port Macquarie Visitor Centre; Tourism Tasmania. Pp 96–97: First Fleet Memorial Gardens; Castle Mountain Farmstay; Tamworth Regional Council; Tourism NSW, photography by Jann Tuxford. Pp 98–99: Lake Crackenback Resort; Thredbo Alpine Resort Centre. Pp 100–101: Stanley Visitor Centre. P 106: South Australian Tourism Commission, photography by Oz, Milton Wordley and Peter Fisher. Pp 108–109: Wardens Food and Wine; Beechworth Visitor Centre. Pp 110–11: Silos Restaurant; Berry Chamber of Commerce and Industry. P 113: Australian War Memorial; National Portrait Gallery; Dawn Drifters. Pp 116–17: Cradle Mountain Huts; Voyages Cradle Mountain Lodge. Pp 118–19: Kingfisher Bay Resort and Village, photography by Peter Meyer and Paul Ewart. P 122: Lavandula Swiss Italian Farm; Cricket Willow. Pp 126–27: Hyams Beach Seaside Cottages; Jervis Bay Kayak Company; Tourism NSW. Pp 128–29: South Australian Tourism Commission, photography by Jon Armstrong, Milton Wordley, David Witts and Neale Winter. Pp 132–33: Azure House, photography by Michael Woods Consulting. Pp 134–35: Hyams Beach Photos, www.paulwhitephotos.com.au. Pp 136–37: Benedictine Community of New Norcia. P 138: Couran Cove Island Resort. Pp 142–43: Eagles Nest Retreat, photography by Dan Fellow; Tourism Tasmania, photography by Geoff Murray, Manabu Konod and Diane Lindsay Stockbridge. P 144–45: World Heritage Cruises; Tourism Tasmania. Pp 146–47: Rosevears Estate and Accommodation; Evandale Village Fair and National Penny Farthing Championship; Tourism Tasmania, photography by Garry Moore. P 149: Surf Coast Tourism, www.visitsurfcoast.com. Pp 150–51: Tourism Victoria; Zoos Victoria; Werribee Park Mansion, photography by Ken Stepnell. Pp 154–55: The Orangerie; South Australian Tourism commission, photography by Milton Wordley and Adam Bruzzone. Pp 156–57: Voyages Ayers Rock Resort; Voyages Logitude 131°. P 158–59: Lilianfels Blue Mountains Resort and Spa; Tourism New South Wales, photography by Peter Lik. P 161: Milton Park Country House Hotel. P 162: Broken Hill Sculpture Symposium. P 164–65: Broome Visitor Centre. P 168: Tourism Queensland, Photography by Peter Lik, Paul Ewart and Barry Goodwin. P 170–71: Daintree Discovery Centre; Voyages Silky Oaks Lodge. P 172–73: Darwin Festival, photography by Peter Eve Monsoon Studio; Mindil Beach Sunset Markets. P 176–77: The Bush Camp. P 178–79: Zirky's. P 181: Club Med Lindeman Island; Tourism Queensland, photography by Peter Lik and Murray Waite & Associates. P 182–83: Voyages Lizard Island Resort. 184–85: Melbourne Sports Tours. P 188–89: Tourism Noosa. Pp 190–91: Phillip Island Nature Park. P 192–93: Robe Visitor Information Centre. Pp 196–97: Wellington Visitors Centre. P 198–99: Voyages Wrotham Park.

AUTUMN

106 ADELAIDE
SA

108 BEECHWORTH
VIC

110 BERRY
NSW

112 CANBERRA
ACT

114 CENTRAL COAST
NSW

116 CRADLE MOUNTAIN
TAS

118 FRASER ISLAND
QLD

120 HAMILTON ISLAND
QLD

122 HEPBURN SPRINGS
VIC

124 HUNTER VALLEY
NSW

126 HYAMS BEACH
NSW

128 LAKE EYRE
SA

130 MELBOURNE
VIC

132 MID NORTH COAST
NSW

134 MURRAY RIVER
SA

136 NEW NORCIA
WA

138 NORTH & SOUTH STRADBROKE
QLD

140 PITTWATER & PALM BEACH
NSW

142 SHEFFIELD
TAS

144 STRAHAN
TAS

146 TAMAR VALLEY
TAS

148 TORQUAY TO APOLLO BAY
VIC

150 WERRIBEE
VIC

WINTER

154 ADELAIDE HILLS
SA

156 AYERS ROCK (ULURU)
NT

158 BLUE MOUNTAINS
NSW

160 BOWRAL
NSW

162 BROKEN HILL
NSW

164 BROOME
WA

166 BYRON HINTERLAND
NSW

168 CAIRNS
QLD

170 DAINTREE
QLD

172 DARWIN
NT

174 ELSEY CREEK STATION
NT

176 FARAWAY BAY
WA

178 HOTHAM
VIC

180 LINDEMAN ISLAND
QLD

182 LIZARD ISLAND
QLD

184 MELBOURNE
VIC

186 NINGALOO
WA

188 NOOSA
QLD

190 PHILLIP ISLAND
VIC

192 ROBE
SA

194 SYDNEY
NSW

196 WELLINGTON
NSW

198 WROTHAM PARK
QLD

INTRODUCTION

Whether you're browsing through this book in a shop right now, or it's become your holiday bible, your interest in it indicates to me that you have an adventurous spirit and an inquisitive mind – my favourite qualities in a travelling companion.

I've been a 'professional traveller' for over ten years now; in love with my job and constantly amazed at the beauty of the world we live in, but it's my own backyard – Australia – that inspires me most. The natural beauty can't be beaten and I'm forever looking forward to my next Aussie trip. The only thing that matches my lust for travel is my desire to share what I've learnt with others.

I must say, writing this book has been an absolute joy. Ok, whopping big challenge too, but there are few topics more pleasant to research than travel, and what a great conversation starter when I've called on the friends I've made through 'Getaway' or speak with passionate travellers from all walks of life, being able to ask all of them this simple question: 'So tell me about your favourite Aussie holiday spots?' The lovely thing is that the reaction is always the same: a cheeky grin slowly spreads across the face, the eyes light up, and then the stories roll out. The fact that I had time to write anything is still a miracle to me, as heaven knows I could have talked till the cows came home!

Now to be able to share those stories and suggestions with you, what bliss. I truly hope this book becomes your favourite holiday guide. That you slowly tick off my travel tips, dog-ear the pages, coffee rim the cover, add your own notes of interest or simply just revel in the pics and dream a little.

Above all, enjoy the journey . . . oh and Bon Voyage!

♡ Catriona Rowntree
xx

TRAVEL BASICS

CHOOSING YOUR DESTINATION

Imagine your dream holiday, where money isn't an issue, nor other people's needs or desires. It is nice to dream, isn't it? But in reality there will always be limitations on every trip. However, if you plan it well, those little hurdles can become part of the fun of getting away.

The first thing I do is make a wish list. I focus on my dream destination (or at least where I can escape to this weekend) then jot down everything that needs to be taken into consideration. Then I start my research and make it happen. A good plan helps get me into the holiday mood, and it turns my dream into a reality.

What's usually on my list? Well, my budget for one; the type of holiday I'm looking for; my travelling companions and their needs; transport options; what I need to pack and what I need to organise before I leave home.

BUDGET

You can go five-star if the wallet permits; if not, remember rates vary, depending on the seasons or day of the week. Weekend rates are usually higher than week days at country and beach properties, and some places insist on a minimum two-night stay. City hotels usually have plenty of weekend specials.

If your getaway is last-minute or your dates are flexible, check discount accommodation websites for real bargains.

TYPE OF HOLIDAY

Where to go obviously depends on what you want from your holiday. Are you looking for rejuvenation or exhilaration, snow or tropical rainforests? Work out what this holiday must include for you. Research is everything here and half the fun is whittling down your holiday options.

TRAVELLING COMPANIONS

You'll need to discuss your budget and the type of holiday with your travelling companions, unless you are planning to surprise them. You also need to be honest about your own, or your companion's, abilities. I found this out while travelling with my Nan. She can't really climb stairs and has difficulty getting into a bathtub, so the shower needs to be a separate cubicle with lower water barriers. You need to take into account all the special needs of your fellow travellers – you can't take children into a casino or dogs into a five-star restaurant! – to make your travels together fun. Here are some extra bits of advice for special cases:

DISABLED TRAVELLERS – When I met Matt Laffan, an expert in travelling with a disability, I picked up some great tips and this also applies to the elderly. Matt's first tip was to research. You need to know what facilities are offered by the hotel, the attractions you want to see and all your transport needs before you leave home. Matt usually finds out how locals in the area he is visiting get around. If your hotel is central to all you want to do, you won't need to rely on transport quite so much. If you need to take special equipment you'll need to know the policy of airlines, etc. for carrying this gear and your tools, which you'll need in case you need to make repairs on the run. Most large hotels can point you to local pharmacies that rent equipment, which might save any transfer problems. The most important tip Matt gave me really applies to everyone: be confident and enthusiastic and just get out there. For more info on Matt and his travels, check out his website: www.mattlaffan.com.au

CHILDREN ON THE MOVE – Involve your children in the planning of the holiday. Tell them how you will get there, where you are staying and how long you'll be away. You might also have to reassure them that their toys back home will be fine while they are away. You'll need to take lots of distractions for them, particularly when on planes or in the car. Take loads of snacks and drinks – when kids are hungry there's no waiting! Maybe offer them a disposable camera to take their own pics of the trip, or a checklist of things they might see on the journey. Don't forget to take extra changes of clothes – just in case. For more ideas, check out www.flyingwithkids.com

PETS TO GO – The good news is that more and more hotels are open to the idea of having pets stay, within reason. If you want to bring along your pet snake, they might just draw the line. Check with the hotel before you go – there is no harm in asking. Airlines have policies about transporting pets, so you need to know these before you rock up to the departure gates. Also take into consideration what to do with Fido when you go out. Most restaurants do not allow dogs on the premises. If they have outdoor seating, though, ask if it's okay for him to curl up under the table. Most museums and art galleries will also say no to pets seeing the exhibits. Again, ask. A friend of mine tucked her Maltese under her arm and walked around an art gallery in Sydney with the owner's blessing. The golden rule is to be fair to your pet. You might want to take them with you, but they may be more comfortable at home with care provided, or in a kennel.

WHAT TO TAKE

My golden rule is: work out what not to take – never take anything you'd be upset to lose and don't overpack. Pile everything into the middle of the room, or on your bed, and work out what is really essential. The more you travel, the more you know that travelling with the smallest possible amount of luggage is the best way to go. I end up halving my original pile and, naturally, that gives me more space for shopping!

TO PACK LIGHTLY

∞ Check what the hotel offers in terms of laundry facilities, robes and toiletries.

∞ Choose clothes that mix and match well to make several great outfits; for example, stick to three colours.

∞ Bring appropriate items for the weather; if you need a coat, take one that will go with all outfits and don't forget the thermals for chilly climes.

∞ Take smaller bottles of toiletries.

∞ Pack your underwear and socks inside your shoes – every bit of space counts.

HOW TO PACK

∞ Avoid taking anything that needs to be ironed.

∞ Compress rolled clothes further by putting them in zip-lock bags and squeezing out excess air; nylon compression bags minimise bulky garments in the same way.

∞ Pack wrinkle-prone clothes in dry-cleaner or zip-lock bags – as the plastic heats up it 'irons' the garments. If your clothes are rumpled on arrival, hang them in the bathroom as you shower – the steam will soften any creases.

- ∞ The best way to pack a backpack is to roll everything tightly.

- ∞ Individual cotton or zip-lock bags can be great for dividing the contents of your pack – you know, underwear, dirty clothes, swimmers . . .

- ∞ A leak-proof toiletries bag should be put in the middle of your pack, surrounded by clothing for extra padding. Make sure you include soap, lip balm and, for camping, loo paper! Avoid glass containers.

THE ESSENTIALS

- ∞ You will need a first aid kit, no matter how basic. I have a standard one from The Travel Doctor – Traveller's Medical and Vaccination Centre. See their website for more information about this: www.tmvc.com.au

- ∞ Don't forget medicine, prescriptions, and letters of medical necessity. I always carry spare ventolin.

- ∞ Write down your bank's helpline number in case your credit card goes missing.

- ∞ You might want to notify your credit card company that you'll be travelling, so they will expect charges from your destination.

- ∞ Don't forget the camera, along with rolls of films or a memory stick and batteries.

DON'T FORGET TO . . .

- ∞ Establish a schedule for periodically contacting people back home and let them know what to do if they don't hear from you.

- ∞ If you have friends or contacts at your destination, double check to see that all contact information is up to date and correct.

- ∞ Know how your travel companion responds in an emergency and discuss various emergency scenarios with him or her.

- ∞ Make an arrangement with a neighbour, friend or relative to check your home periodically, collect mail and care for plants (indoors and outdoors).

- ∞ Arrange for someone to start your car during very cold or very hot weather.

- ∞ Arrange boarding for your pets.

- ∞ If travelling by car, get the car checked and have the oil changed. Don't wait until the last minute, it may take time to get an appointment and parts may need to be ordered. You also want some time to drive around town and make sure that whatever they fixed stays fixed.

- ∞ Pay bills that will come due while you are away.

- ∞ Cancel or hold your newspaper delivery.

- ∞ Turn off or unplug unnecessary equipment in the house, like the television.

SPRING

THE BAROSSA

Without a doubt, this is one of Australia's richest and best-known viticultural regions. But my fascination with the area lies in its history and the hardship that has gone into creating the world-class wines. For me, the Barossa is just as much a cultural experience as a wine-tasting holiday.

The first German settlers arrived in 1839 and today it still feels like a pocket of Europe plopped in the middle of the state's fascinating arid landscape. Talk to the owners about their family history – some have been here for six generations – and you learn stories of remarkable faith and courage. You sip, let them chat, and I promise it'll enhance the flavour.

I recommend touring the area in style, in a vintage car with Auburn Tours. One of the big pluses to this means of travel: you don't have to worry about being over the limit as you have a responsible driver on hand who is also an expert on the area. It's a great way to get around.

For accommodation I love AL-RU Farm and its Garden Pavilion Bed and Breakfast. Apart from being central to both Adelaide and the many, many vineyards of the Barossa, it is home to one of the most beautiful gardens I've ever seen. Wander among the bursting beds, notebook in hand, with owner Ruth Irving and you'll be inspired. She is so talented; put simply, she took a basic farm on the outskirts of the city and turned it into a French Provincial mansion. Glorious on every level.

MY TIP

Ruth from AL-RU Farm is also an antiques dealer, so check out the barn filled with her latest international finds – they're all for sale, so you can start/add to your own collection!

GETTING THERE

Around one hour's drive north of Adelaide, depending on which way you drive there. There are heaps of tours from Adelaide and within the region.

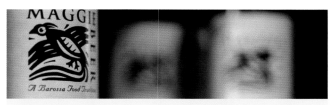

WHAT TO DO WHEN IN THE AREA

∞ See the magnificent chateaux, such as Yaldara, Tanunda and Seppeltsfield, and Barossa's parklands, where there are more than 20,000 rose bushes on show.

∞ Be tempted by Maggie Beer's farm and shop near Nuriootpa and stock up on her gourmet products and award-winning books.

∞ Sample the goods at the Barossa Farmers' Market; every Saturday morning from 7.30 am to 11.30 am.

∞ Tell your secrets to the Whispering Wall – the Barossa Reservoir retaining wall that has unique acoustic effects – words whispered at one end of the dam wall can be heard at the other, more than 100 metres away – but be careful who's listening!

∞ Go online and find out what gardens in the area are open for inspection as part of the Australian Open Garden Scheme.

∞ And don't forget, for even more vineyards the Clare Valley is not too far away!

BAROSSA WINE AND VISTOR INFORMATON CENTRE
66–68 Murray Street, Tanunda 5352
P: **08 8563 0600** W: **www.barossa-region.org**

AUBURN TOURS
8 Collins Street, Angaston 5353
P: **08 8564 2144** W: **www.auburntours.com.au**

AL-RU FARM
Golden Grove Road, One Tree Hill 5114
P: **08 8280-7353** W: **www.ruthirving.com.au**

AUSTRALIAN OPEN GARDEN SCHEME
South Australian Coordinator
P: **08 8388 0119** W: **www.opengarden.org.au**

OR VISIT: **www.southaustralia.com**

BEDARRA ISLAND

Many islands in Australia claim to be the ultimate. Indeed, they are gorgeous; however, if you're after the most exclusive, the most luxurious island, for me there's only one place that wins hands down . . . Bedarra. If I have to define why, I would quite simply say it's the privacy. True, the design, the cuisine, the amenities and service are all of an international standard, but what makes a sporting star (no names, no pack drill) choose here, of all places, to get married? The privacy. Royalty, movie stars – they could go anywhere – yet this is the playground they all want to immerse in. No daytrippers please, no gawking staff thank you, no prying eyes here. Bedarra quietly leaves its guests be. Pure relaxation.

There are loads of complimentary activities to enjoy, like catamarans and paddle skis on call and the self-guided walks along nature trails through lush tropical rainforest. I also like the fact that there is actually a choice of accommodation – not too much to fear unwanted observation, though. Voyages offer 16 gorgeous villas (which means never more than 32 guests) and the Bedarra Island Villa & Studio on Doorila Beach provides private accommodation that's favoured by the more creative types.

Doorila lays claim to being the best beach on the island but any on this tropical paradise provide hypnotic views of the reef. No one here feels the need to scream the island's virtues . . . why bother? They all know this is the ultimate.

MY TIP

At the resort, no whim goes unfulfilled. Green ant ice-cream is the most unusual request to date – I dare you to set the staff a challenge.

GETTING THERE

East of Mission Beach, the only way in is to fly from Cairns to Dunk Island, and then catch the 20-minute boat transfer to Bedarra.

WHAT TO DO WHEN IN THE AREA

∞ For the sailor in you, hop on a catamaran, sailboard, paddle ski or motorised dinghy to explore beaches and neighbouring islands.

∞ For the splashers, go swimming, snorkelling or perhaps even fishing.

∞ For land lovers, there are gourmet picnic hampers for beachside lunches, self-guided island walks and nature trails, or tennis and a gymnasium for the more energetic.

∞ For those who want to relax inside, each room is stocked with DVD/CD players, books, games and a CD library.

∞ You're on holiday, have a great time.

BEDARRA ISLAND VILLA & STUDIO
P: 02 9331 2881 W: www.bedarraisland.com.au

VOYAGES BEDARRA ISLAND
P: 1300 134 044/02 8296 801 W: www.bedarraisland.com

OR VISIT: www.queenslandholidays.com.au

BRISBANE

Didn't Brisbane used to feel like a big ol' country town? Not any more. This place is loud and proud, reaping in the awards, shaking up the other capitals in the 'best of' stakes. Fashion, food, clubs and hotels . . . they're winners. Is it the climate, the laid-back cool, the lack of pressure and pretension? I dunno, but I know I like it and the atmosphere in this city today is buzzing.

As far as food goes, for the best modern Australian food try Restaurant Two. It's always packed, with guests no doubt lured by the fact that it's Brissy's first restaurant to be given three red stars by *Gourmet Traveller*, among other accolades. Co-owner David Pugh has a totally unique cooking style and Michael Conrad defines charm.

Another award winner is the Treasury Casino. I adore the high ceilings in this century-old establishment. A fine example of Edwardian Baroque architecture with big lovely rooms, no two the same. Hard to imagine that it was once, as its name suggests, the home of the government's treasury. Oh, and it's neatly placed smack dab in the middle of the city.

For more fun, head to The Valley. Yep, it's been given a spruce up and is now home to great bars and clubs. I braved the door witch at Family and, although she thought my dress daggy, I loved the venue's four levels of differently themed bars and dance floors. Ever changing, always cool, there's an air of confidence in Brisbane today that I've not detected before. This city has truly come into its own.

WHAT TO DO WHEN IN THE AREA

∞ Check out the Riverfestival, a major annual community and environmental celebration that kicks off spring and focuses on the city's signature natural landmark, the Brisbane River.

∞ Relish in great places to eat and drink during the balmy evenings at South Bank, The Valley (including Chinatown), Caxton Street, West End, Bulimba, James Street, Emporium, Sandgate Road and Albion, among others.

∞ Visit two great botanic gardens, one in Toowong, the other in the heart of the city.

∞ Trek to the top of Mount Cootha for a fabulous view of the city during the day or night.

∞ Stroll along the riverside walk at New Farm.

∞ Rummage among the stalls at the South Bank markets on the weekend.

MY TIP

For shopping with a difference, have a look at Latrobe Terrace in Paddington – great vintage clothing!

GETTING THERE

As a state captial, access is via plane, rail, bus or car. Brisbane lies about halfway along the eastern seaboard, for those that don't know.

OUR BRISBANE
W: www.ourbrisbane.com

RESTAURANT TWO
2 Edward Street, Brisbane 4000
P: 07 3210 0600 W: www.restaurant2.com.au

CONRAD TREASURY
Top of Queen Street Mall, Brisbane 4001
P: 07 3306 8888 W: www.conrad.com.au

RIVERFESTIVAL BRISBANE
Level 1, Allgas Building, Stanley St Plaza, South Bank 4101
P: 07 3846 7444 W: www.riverfestival.com.au

OR VISIT: www.queenslandholidays.com.au

BYRON BAY

How to sum up the enigmatic allure of this town? The natural beauty, where hinterland meets the sea; the rolling surf; the youth and cafe cultures? This once sleepy shire is famous for its creativity, independence and vibrant energy. There aren't too many places where you can take a dip at an exquisite beach, go shopping in your togs, do a belly dancing class in the street and roll on to a fantastic restaurant.

First, go and watch the sunrise at Australia's most easterly point, the Lighthouse – it's the thing to do. Then wander down to Watego's. This exclusive real estate (once a banana plantation farmed by Mr Watego) is home to the glamorous Rae's. When I stayed there I shared the hotel with Keith Richards and his family – so cool! The other hot place is the Byron Bay Villa – absolute privacy and to-die-for views.

Then walk around to the Beach Cafe on Clarks to plan your day: a spa, yoga class, surf school, exploration of the hinterland or . . . a flake on the beach. But be prepared for the nightlife, it's huge. The streets come alive with music and glowing individuals. You can watch all the action from The Balcony or Cocomangas. For live music go to 'The Rails' or the Corner Pub. Dish is a happening restaurant and new bars and dining spots are opening all the time.

It's hard to sum Byron up; it's a place that is constantly changing, yet what we love about it – beaches, buzz and beautiful characters – never seems to alter.

MY TIP

Spend time with true locals: the resident dolphin pod. The Byron Bay Adventure Company can take you out into the middle of them on a kayak – an emotional experience.

GETTING THERE

Byron Bay is conveniently located close to Brisbane (175 km), making it easy to get to. Trains and buses go there, of course, and there are airports at Coolangatta and Ballina.

WHAT TO DO WHEN IN THE AREA

∞ For the earth-bound, there are national parks, eco tours, bush safaris, markets, tennis and golf courses . . . just pick one and go.

∞ For water-lovers, there are diving and surfing tours, kiteboarding, swimming, kayaking, fishing . . . get wet!

∞ For high flyers, there's sky-diving, gliding or ballooning . . . going up!

∞ Then there are loads of mind, body and spirit adventures to be had.

RAE'S ON WATEGO'S
8 Marine Parade, Watego's Beach 2481
P: 02 6685 5366 W: www.raes.com.au

BYRON BAY VILLA
Watego's Beach 2481
P: 02 9331 2881

BALCONY BAR AND RESTAURANT
3 Lawson Street, Byron Bay 2481
P: 02 6680 9666

COCOMANGAS
32 Jonson Street, Byron Bay 2481
P: 02 6685 8493

RAILWAY FRIENDLY BAR
Railway Station, Jonson Street, Byron Bay 2481
P: 02 6685 7662

THE BEACH HOTEL
Cnr Jonson and Bay streets, Byron Bay 2481
P: 02 6685 6402

DISH RESTAURANT RAW BAR
Cnr Jonson and Marvel streets, Byron Bay 2481
P: 02 6685 5388

OR VISIT: www.visitnsw.com.au

CANBERRA

It took me a while to figure Canberra out. There was a time when I'd want to stop people on the roundabouts and ask them, 'Where are you going? What's there to do?' Well, constant 'Getaway' assignments have solved this dilemma; now I'm a fan and I sing its praises. So here goes.

During spring you'll see the capital truly blossom, literally. Floriade, one of Australia's greatest garden festivals, takes centre stage and has the city bursting with colour and fragrance. I'm amazed at the precision timing that goes into planning the 30-day festival. Each day a new bloom. I love the Rhododendrons that take the final bow, but it'll have you smiling throughout. Ten points.

I also think Canberra is brilliant for children. My gosh, ten years ago I would never have said that, but that was before the National Museum went all groovy on us. The design of the building has barely a straight line and they've been able to capture the hearts and minds of young people by being interactive. As has Questacon, an interactive science centre that had me occupied for hours . . . oh, and my young friends, too.

My favourite Canberra experience, though, has to be the behind-the-scenes tour of the National Zoo & Aquarium. Brilliant. I actually fed a chicken wing to a tiger and had a minor altercation with a capuchin monkey after upsetting him with direct eye contact. I survived, clearly. So, Canberra really does cater for all ages. Who knew!

WHAT TO DO WHEN IN THE AREA

∞ Walk, run or cycle lakeside after visiting Floriade – it's the perfect compliment.

∞ A trip to Parliament House is a must. Afterall, this is the point of the capital.

∞ See my suggestions for Canberra in Winter – there's so much more to this place.

MY TIP

Canberra was one of the first cities to offer balloon flights, right over the capital. A dawn trip is truly a bird's-eye view.

GETTING THERE

The nation's capital is about a three-hour drive from Sydney. You can drive, fly, or catch the train or bus into Canberra. You could even walk there if you're so inclined!

CAPE LEVEQUE

Talk about a bunch of show-offs. No sooner had I arrived on board our catamaran, still in my city duds, my mouth agape at the true aqua-coloured waters surrounding me, when a pod of humpback whales leapt into the air, pulling out every trick in the bag. Nice welcoming party and, trust me, you can never fully appreciate a whale's majesty until it dances in front of you. Life changing. If you're the sort of tourist that wants marine life on tap, get thee to Cape Leveque at the Kimberley.

When you're there I vote you head out on a smaller boat for a more intimate experience. You can probably chat to a marine biologist one-on-one and have fabulous gourmet food catered to your liking. Although I have to admit, when we were on board our catamaran we simply popped a line into the water and minutes later were hauling up the giant Spanish mackerel for dinner. At night we slept on deck, under a brilliant canopy of stars, and listened to the whales calling to each other. Just magical.

I was amazed that during the week I was there, cruising among the Buccaneer and Bonaparte Archipelagoes, I rarely caught sight of another vessel. The only time I chatted to another traveller was at Crocodile Creek (don't be put off by this name; it's a natural spring, high up from the water's edge, and it is safe and refreshing to swim in). The Kimberley is not for the faint-hearted, though. I lost count of the amount of crocs I spotted and found it quite odd to be surrounded by exquisite waters that were off limits due to these awesome creatures. But those waters also cast a spell on me, too good to turn my back on, and I can't wait to return and continue my adventures.

WHAT TO DO WHEN IN THE AREA

- ∞ Book a flight and see this fabulous landscape from the air.
- ∞ Breathe in the sights from the Cape Leveque Lighthouse on the tip of the peninsula and admire the vibrant colours of the white sands, red earth and blue sea.
- ∞ Go inland and explore the rugged outback landscape.
- ∞ Visit nearby Derby, Windjana National Park, Drysdale River Station, El Questro Wilderness Park and Kununurra.

MY TIP

The Kimberley is always singular, so don't pronounce it as a plural. This goose learnt that one the hard way.

GETTING THERE

It's in the Kimberley region, on the tip of Dampier Peninsula, about 220 km north of Broome on an unsealed road, so you'll need a 4WD (about three and a half hours to drive). Lots of fly/drive tours and scenic flights and charter boats can be booked from Broome.

AUSTRALIA'S NORTH WEST TOURISM
W: www.kimberleytourism.com

KING LEOPOLD AIR
Shop 7B, Johnny Chi Lane, Broome 6725
P: 08 9193 7155   W: www.kingleopoldair.com.au

OR VISIT: www.westernaustralia.com

DANDENONGS

The Dandenongs are an enchanting place. The trees, the fresh air, the village feel. It has that certain something that lifts the spirits. Maybe because I arrived in the early morning mist, my memories of it have this kind of magical quality. At night you almost feel as though you're in a tiny European hamlet as the pretty lights twinkle and the restaurants are full of warming chat and laughter. The only complaint I hear from other travellers who visit the area is that they don't allocate enough time to see it all.

The area has a reputation for Devonshire teas but the reality is that here there is a very eclectic mix of people, restaurants and shops. I stayed at Como Cottages which, sadly for this lone reporter, is unbelievably romantic. I'm delighted to say, though, that business is booming and they're booked out virtually every weekend. Oh, and they have also bought the old service station and now offer massages, pilates and local arts and crafts on site.

Shopping highlights are found in Olinda, at Mountain Ash Trading for gifts and at Verve for beautiful body products. Food wise, Ranges and Credo are great contemporary restaurants and the Pig & Whistle is an old English pub with a brilliant atmosphere.

The Dandenongs is also a great spot for children. The Puffing Billy steam train cannot be missed, and there are the carvings and sculptures at William Ricketts Sanctuary. By the way, the Devonshire teas in town are still awesome.

MY TIP

The Dandenongs are the place to experience the true seasons, but spring is my favourite. This is when the flowers at the National Rhododendron Gardens are in full bloom.

GETTING THERE

East from Melbourne along the Moondah Highway, about an hour's drive from the city. The train goes there, as do buses.

WHAT TO DO WHEN IN THE AREA

∞ Visit all the little villages; they are delightful: Olinda, Sassafras, Belgrave, Emerald, Gembrook.

∞ Don't miss a trip on Puffing Billy; departs and returns from Belgrave.

∞ Explore the national parks and the many other parks and gardens in the area.

∞ Hang out with the locals in pubs that have distinctive personalities.

DANDENONG RANGES AND
KNOX VISITOR INFORMATION CENTRE
1211 Burwood Highway, Upper Ferntree Gully 3156
P: 03 9758 7522/1800 645 505

COMO COTTAGE ACCOMMODATION
1465 Mt Dandenong Tourist Road, Olinda 3788
P: 03 9751 2264 W: www.comocottages.com

PUFFING BILLY
Old Monbulk Road, Belgrave 3160
P: 03 9754 6800 W: www.puffingbilly.com.au

WILLIAM RICKETTS SANCTUARY
Mount Dandenong Tourist Road, Mount Dandenong 3767
P: 13 1963 W: www.parkweb.vic.gov.au

NATIONAL RHODODENDRON GARDENS
The Georgian Road, Olinda 3788
P: 03 9751 1980/13 19 63 W: www.parkweb.vic.gov.au

OR VISIT: www.visitvictoria.com

FLINDERS ISLAND

For all its wild and woolly reputation, its lonesome shores and dramatic landscapes, my time on Flinders was one of tranquility, peace and relaxation. I'd answered the call to attend a health retreat that scorned boot camps, offered hearty food and organic wine (my first ever sampling and it's good) and exercise when the mood took me, not when I was ordered to. The unassuming Healing Dreams is a small retreat where you can just check out of life for a brief spell, get a bit healthy, and basically just chill in an awesome natural environment.

They say there's an energy exuding from the pink and grey granite cliffs of Strzelecki/Killiecrankie. I don't know if that's true but I felt an instant calm here. The imposing cliffs give way to green rolling farmland, down to the coast where rocks are covered in vivid lichen that changes colour as the sun hits. The rocks spill out to the sea where many a ship has floundered and where now divers devour the sites. Fishermen love these waters for their abundant sea life, but I loved wandering the coast on my own. Over 100 beaches to explore, and even with 900 people living on the island I barely saw another soul.

Whitemark is the major town, Lady Barron and Emita smaller communities. You'll find beautiful jewellery made by the local women in some of the shops. Try cycling through the towns or go for a climb in this whopping big backyard. But definitely end the day with a soak in the hot tub and maybe a chat in front of the roaring fire.

Maybe I was spoilt, but the weather for my stay was perfect. Absolute peace, and yes, my jeans were a little looser by the end of my stay. A double victory.

GETTING THERE

This isle is about 20 km north of Cape Portland (northeast tip of Tasmania) in the Bass Strait. It is one of the Furneaux group of islands. Flights and charter boats depart regularly from Tasmania, and tours and car rental are available on the island to get you from A to B.

WHAT TO DO WHEN IN THE AREA

∞ Join the locals at the Flinders Island Show in October.

∞ Wander the foreshore while you beachcomb and inspect the shipwrecks.

∞ Discover the wildlife, including mutton birds and seals – the first settlers here were sealers – in the wild or at the sanctuary.

∞ Be energetic: go bushwalking, cycling, diving or fishing.

MY TIP

Whether or not you join in on the painting classes offered at Healing Dreams, take a sketch pad with you; you'll want to remember the views. They are inspirational.

A FLINDERS ISLANDERS' WEBSITE
W: **www.focusonflinders.com.au**

HEALING DREAMS RETREAT
PO Box 125, Whitemark, Flinders Island 7255
P: **03 6359 4588**   W: **www.healingdreams.com.au**

OR VISIT: **www.discovertasmania.com.au**

HAWKESBURY RIVER

Looking for somewhere to go with that someone special? The Hawkesbury has got to be on your list. If you don't feel the love here, honey, you're just not trying.

Let me set the scene. You're picked up by a small boat from the mainland and ferried across to your private boathouse, cottage or plain old love shack, as I like to call it. There are quite a few choices around here, with varying personalities and designs, so something to suit everyone and their budget. Some have decks that spill right on to the water, hammocks to hang about in, romantic bedrooms with views either to the water or up to trees and native bush behind you. There are even those fully equipped with CD/DVD/VCR players and well-stocked kitchens. All you need to do is light a candle, pop a cork and don't forget the oysters – they're harvested in this area, so guaranteed to be fresh.

Hawkesbury Cruises runs the M.V. *Emily Melvey*, a family-owned and operated charter vessel. On board you can cruise the lower Hawkesbury in style while you learn about the history of the area, including Governor Philips' first contact with the native Dhrung tribe in 1788.

One outing I do insist you take while in the area is to Peats Bite. It is one of greater Sydney's best restaurants. It's a classic and so successful they only open for the warmer months of the year. Divine gourmet food, ripper views and feel free to get up and sing with the owners. This is the Hawkesbury, no rules, so let the mood take you. I insist.

WHAT TO DO WHEN IN THE AREA

∞ Cruise the waterways of Pittwater, Cowan Waters, Broken Bay and Hawkesbury River on a houseboat or tinny.

∞ Pack a picnic and visit Dangar Island and the river settlements of Bar Point, Milsons Passage, Coba Point and Berowra Waters, or the many coves in the national parks.

∞ Pop into the oyster farms in the area, learn a bit and indulge in the freshest produce.

MY TIP

Come here during the week as you will almost certainly have the place to yourself.

GETTING THERE

On the northern edge of Sydney; travel to Brooklyn, about one hour's drive north of Sydney. You can also train it, or catch a bus.

HAWKESBURY CRUISES
P: 02 9985 9900   W: www.hawkesburycruises.com.au

PEATS BITE RESTAURANT
Sunny Corner, Hawkesbury River, Brooklyn 2083
P: 02 9985 9040   W: www.peatsbite.com

HAWKESBURY ESCAPES
Hawkesbury River Marina, Mckell Park, Brooklyn 2083
P: 02 9985 7888   W: www.hawkesburyriver.com

THE BOAT HOUSE ON HAWKESBURY
Hawkesbury River, Brooklyn 2083
P: 02 9985 8505   W: www.boathouseonhawkesbury.com.au

OR VISIT: www.visitnsw.com.au

ILLAWARRA REGION

I've always loved the train trip from Central Station to Wollongong. You just leave the chaos of the city and arrive in a laid-back surf centre. On the way the train snakes around the mountains, past small towns, coastal rainforests, and offers the best views out to the crashing waves of the Pacific. However, these days the thing to do is the Grand Pacific Drive. Starting from the Royal National Park (or Shoalhaven Heads, depending on which way you're travelling), it's much safer than the old road and an easy trip from Sydney. The Sea Cliff Bridge, at 665 metres high, is pretty impressive but I wonder how this new road will alter the nearby towns? I'd never heard of Wombarra, but it's now home to the coolest beach house on the coast. Designed by Ed Lippmann, it's modern and laidback. I'm loving the state-of-the-art kitchen, and the views just don't get any better. Not bad, not bad at all.

Kiama is my favourite beach in the Illawarra, though. Set just back from the water, the little cottages are great for lunch and shopping and you're only a short drive away from the beautiful green hills of the Jamberoo Valley, where I recently took a cooking class at Elise Pascoe's. Apparently we whipped up something amazing. I just remember talking my head off with one of our most famous and respected food writers and generally having a ball. I know Elise could live anywhere in the world, but this coastal area is where she chooses to call home. Lucky girl.

WHAT TO DO WHEN IN THE AREA

∞ Download maps from Tourism Wollongong and do the foot-power tour of the city (takes two to three hours); there's also a map for cycling the region.

∞ So many places, not enough time! See the Kiama Blowhole, Bulli Tops, Minamurra Rainforest, Lake Illawarra and Shellharbour for starters.

∞ For an action packed arrival, skydive right on to North Beach in Wollongong – the views are great.

MY TIP

Kiama wins hands down for the best seafood around – so fresh it's virtually straight off the boat. You buy it from a shack that's basically on the beach and devour it in the nearby park. Don't forget the tartare sauce.

ILLAWARRA TOURIST CENTRES
W: www.southcoast.com.au/illawarra

TOURISM WOLLONGONG
W: www.tourismwollongong.com

WOMBARRA BEACH HOUSE
P: 02 9331 2881 W: www.contemporaryhotels.com.au

ELISE PASCOE INTERNATIONAL COOKING SCHOOL
Jamberoo NSW 2533
P: 02 4236 1666 W: www.cookingschool.com.au

SKYDIVE THE BEACH
Stuart Park, North Beach Wollongong 2500
P: 02 4225 8444/4225 7111 W: www.skydivethebeach.com

OR VISIT: www.visitnsw.com.au

GETTING THERE

Wollongong is only 85 km (just over an hour's drive) from Sydney. Access is also via bus and rail.

KANGAROO VALLEY

It's always a bit exciting as you approach Kangaroo Valley: you drive across through the gorgeous towns of the Southern Highlands and south coast, wind your way through rainforest, hopes building at each turn, and then this beautiful country village just opens up in front of you. There's so much going on here as more and more people tree-change, moving from the city with their 'have computer will travel' philosophy. Kangaroo Valley can't possibly still hold the reputation of Australia's best-kept secret because so many people have now discovered how wonderful this area is. The pub, the classic old fruit-and-veg store, the funky cafes and the cool shopping. What's not to love?

I'm very impressed with a place called Skyfarm, a retreat literally found at the top of a mountain that is sometimes shrouded with clouds. The owner is an architect and he was clearly inspired by his natural surroundings. While the private haven has a simple design, it highlights the magnetic view, straight out across the Moreton National Park to Jervis Bay, with a backdrop of thick (almost spooky) rainforest. I really couldn't take my eyes off the vista. Actually, I was smiling before I'd even entered the gates, where a team of wombats with attitude turned out to greet me. They hung out with us the whole time, sharing the limelight with the odd roo and native bird. Don't ever cross a wombat, by the way, they're quite narky, territorial and they growl. Not a sweet bone to be found in their chunky little bodies. Bless 'em.

WHAT TO DO WHEN IN THE AREA

∞ What's not to do?

∞ Hire a canoe or kayak, play a spot of golf, go hiking or bushwalking, or even cycling.

∞ Visit the Pioneer Farm Museum.

∞ Explore the Moreton National Park and Fitzroy Falls.

∞ Admire the charming Hampden Bridge, then stroll into the village for afternoon tea and browse through the antique shops and art galleries.

MY TIP

In early spring the air might still be a bit nippy, so make sure you have a wonderful bottle of red on hand to warm the cockles.

KANGAROO VALLEY TOURIST ASSOCIATION
W: www.kangaroovalleytourist.asn.au

SKYFARM
Tallowa Dam Road, Kangaroo Valley 2577
P: 02 4465 1945 W: www.skyfarm.com.au

PIONEER FARM MUSEUM
Moss Vale Road, Kangaroo Valley 2577
P: 02 4465 1306 W: www.pioneerfarmmuseum.org

OR VISIT: www.visitnsw.com.au

GETTING THERE

In the Shoalhaven, Kangaroo Valley is only a two hours' drive from Sydney or Canberra.

KING ISLAND

I'm a savoury girl myself. A cheese platter is my idea of heaven, so it stands to reason that King Island is my kinda place. Famous the world over for producing mouth-watering cheeses and cream, I was immediately drawn to the main dairy where you are able to sample, learn and buy over 13 different varieties. I remember purposefully stuffing up my lines while filming just so I could keep gobbling down more cheese. 'Roaring Forties' is quite a tongue twister, you know!

To be fair, cheese is not the only produce of note: there are elephant oysters, king crab, grass-fed beef and crayfish. I'd say the legendary produce of this island is due to the happy cows, but a King Island farmer would let you know that they can claim perhaps the cleanest rainfall in the world. Clean rain, exceptional grass, happy cows . . . on it goes.

The island also delights travellers with its white sandy beaches, fairy penguins, diving and fishing. I was fascinated by the calcified forest, around 7,000 years old, and by the Cape Wickham and Currie Lighthouse history. We've all heard about the perilous waters around here from the stories of the Sydney to Hobart Yacht Race, yet long before that contest many a ship met its sad demise on these rocks. The lighthouse cottage is now a museum housing artefacts from those very ships. It's very moving.

Today, tourism holds the promise of so much for the island. A small touch I loved was each tourist being met and farewelled at the airport, making for happy tourists AND happy cows!

WHAT TO DO WHEN IN THE AREA

∞ Dine out on the finest, locally produced food; it's a given.

∞ Follow the shipwreck trail along the rugged coastline and marvel that there weren't more.

∞ Wander through the local arts and crafts outlets where you'll find wonderful gifts.

MY TIP

Travel guilt-free around the island by bicycle. The island has no traffic lights, no traffic, no pollution, no stress, so it's a real treat and a pleasurable way to travel.

GETTING THERE

King Island is bang in the middle of the Bass Strait, about an hour's flight from Melbourne and Launceston.

KING ISLAND TOURIST INC.
George Street, Currie, King Island 7256
P: 1800 645 014   W: www.kingisland.org.au

BAUDINS
Naracoopa Esplanade, Naracoopa, King Island 7256
P: 03 6461 1110   W: www.kingisland.org.au

WAVE WATCHER
Unit 18, Beach Road, Currie, King Island 7256
P: 03 6462 1517

OR VISIT: www.discovertasmania.com.au

KINGS CANYON

Uluru gets so much attention, but for my money the true crown of the Red Centre belongs to Kings Canyon, a magnificent sandstone chasm that plunges 270 metres from top to tail. It's dramatic, varied, and aside from its visual beauty and alluring history, travellers are brilliantly catered for while staying here.

Eerie, beautiful, rugged, red rock – 300 million years of water and wind erosion have gone into creating this sight, and it probably all started out as a mere fracture in the stone. You can see the canyon in several ways: wander along the creek walk, commit yourself to the steep incline up to the canyon's rim, or chopper over and into it. The aerial view offers you a whole new way to appreciate the full scale and grandeur of the chasm and also to check out the rugged surroundings. I sampled all three and do admit to suffering a bit of vertigo while I was looking from the rim down to the base. I can't really say I felt like I was standing on the edge of the world because I had to lie flat on my tummy to peer over the edge!

Three Aboriginal communities still live in the park and the original custodians are the Luritja people. Their presence is abundantly evident as they still live, hunt and collect food here. So for a traveller it's a constant learning experience when you talk to the locals. We're also a bit spoilt by the Kings Canyon Resort. They offer every level of accommodation, from spa bath suites to arguably the Territory's best camping grounds. Everyone staying here can share the sunset via a wonderfully positioned viewing platform and I recommend the gastronomical treat, the Sounds of Firelight dinner – champagne at sunset followed by a four-course menu.

Sensitive, respectful, professional and forward-thinking tourism at its best. Well worth the crown.

GETTING THERE

Three hours from both Alice Springs and Uluru; fly to either destination, then hire a car or catch a coach transfer.

WHAT TO DO WHEN IN THE AREA

∞ For a racey outback adventure, explore Kings Creek Station by camel or four-wheel quad bike. You'll probably need a lie in the spa afterwards!

∞ If you're driving, don't forget to stop at Standley Chasm, Ellery Creek and Ormiston Gorge, among all the other incredible geological wonders.

∞ Check out the marine fossils of the Lost City. It's a trip back in time.

∞ Take note of the age-old cycad ferns, red river gums and all the other species of plant that survive off the little bit of water captured in the rock.

MY TIP

If you take up the chance to do an aerial tour, ask to fly over the domes of the Lost City and the Garden of Eden; they're equally beautiful.

VOYAGES KINGS CANYON RESORT
Watarrka National Park, Luritja Road, Kings Canyon
P: 08 8956 7442 W: www.kingscanyonresort.com.au

PROFESSIONAL HELICOPTER SERVICES
PO Box 348, Ayers Rock 0872
P: 08 8956 2003 W: www.phs.com.au

OR VISIT: www.tourismnt.com.au

LONGFORD

There's always something to lure me back to Longford. I have a mild crush on this Georgian village, which dates back to 1813. It's home to one of the most intact heritage landscapes in Australia; it's also a brilliant town to tour by bicycle. Kick your trip off in Launceston and spend a couple of days taking in the patchwork fields, hawthorn hedges and charming old farmhouses on the road to Longford. It almost feels like you're back in the motherland – the Queen did choose to visit nearby Woolmers Estate, which adds to that mood (Liz was apparently very impressed and she had tea with the locals while she was there).

Surely Tassie's finest and most historic family estate, I'm positive Woolmers is haunted by one of the six generations of the Archer family who have lived there. No doubt they'd feel right at home as it's still brimming with their art, furniture, clothing, photographs and vintage cars. It's like they never left. Personally, I love the gardens, and do try to see the nearby homestead of Brickendon with its little chapel, blacksmith shop, etc. Farm life just keeps rolling on by.

Try to also get out on the water while at Longford. I loved my canoe trip, where I spotted the odd shy platypus, black swan and other bird life. If you're into fly-fishing (and why wouldn't you be?) this area is fast gaining a reputation for hauling in both rainbow and brown trout. The local guides pop you into a raft and you drift by some of the state's most beautiful countryside.

MY TIP

Check out the National Rose Garden at Woolmers Estate. It's a complete collection of all 19 of the rose families, one of only three such gardens in the nation.

GETTING THERE

About 24 km (a 25-minute drive) southwest of Launceston; two hours from Hobart by car.

WHAT TO DO WHEN IN THE AREA

∞ Don't leave without admiring all the historic buildings here: Christ Church, Queen's Arms, Blenheim Hotel, Longford Library, Longford House, Old Norley, Brickendon, Northbury.

∞ Only nine kilometres out of Longford is the Woodstock Lagoon Wildlife Sanctuary, a safe harbour for nesting and breeding water birds – great for birdwatchers.

∞ Hop on a bicycle and set out to enjoy the green, lush scenery.

∞ Heaps of walking trails, or for more regal fare, take a spot of tea in a village atmosphere.

HERITAGE CENTRE
1b Marlborough Street, Longford 7301
P: 03 6391 1181

WOOLMERS ESTATE
Woolmers Lane, Longford 7301
P: 03 6391 2230 W: www.woolmers.com.au

OR VISIT: www.discovertasmania.com.au

LORD HOWE ISLAND

Imagine an island paradise so exquisite, so pristine, with a collection of plants, animals and marine life so rare that it's World Heritage listed; yet you can flick on the radio and listen to Triple J while catching up on the goss in that day's mainland newspaper. Welcome to Lord Howe, just a two-hour flight from Sydney but miles from worries.

This place has a strange dichotomy between feeling 'a world away' while still connected to sassy NSW. Protection is the key to its success in keeping the hordes at bay; only 400 guests are allowed on the island at any one time and the locals are devoted to keeping it in as mint condition as possible. So forget your love affair with the car, take a bike and revel in this island's exceptional natural beauty.

For my money, Capella Lodge is the funkiest place to stay on the island. It has a prime view of the soaring Mount Gower and its $1.5 million upgrade has created an ultra luxurious resort with private suites, a spa and restaurant. You can end your 'hectic' day with a cocktail at The Makambo Bar while watching the sun set over the dramatic coast and towering volcanic peaks. It doesn't get any better than this.

You'll be floored by the island's unspoilt grandeur. It is fringed by the most southern coral reef in the world, containing 400 species of fish and 90 species of coral, some of which are found nowhere else in the world. Ned's Beach was voted the cleanest in Australia – so this is the place where water babies, nature lovers and old romantic fools will find their paradise!

WHAT TO DO WHEN IN THE AREA

∞ Just chill – the pace can be as slow as you like.

∞ Go all natural, join a tour and go birdwatching or fishing.

∞ Dive in – the water's divinely clean and there are loads of fish to meet and coral to explore.

∞ Set your aim high and clamber up Mount Gower.

MY TIP

In the afternoon, head to Ned's Beach on the east coast to hand-feed hundreds of tropical fish that come right up to you for a nibble. They're not shy.

GETTING THERE

A two-hour flight from Sydney, Brisbane or Coffs Harbour.

VISITOR INFORMATION CENTRE
Lagoon Road, Lord Howe Island 2898
P: 02 6563 2114/1800 240 937 W: www.lordhoweisland.info

CAPELLA LODGE
Lagoon Road, Lord Howe Island 2898
P: 02 9918 4355 W: www.lordhowe.com

PINETREES RESORT HOTEL
Lagoon Road, Lord Howe Island 2898
P: 02 6563 2177 W: www.pinetrees.com.au

OR VISIT: www.visitnsw.com.au

MELBOURNE

I love shopping in Melbourne for its European sophistication and the Melburnian passion for food. A spree here is always punctuated by cool cafe stops.

In Chapel Street the locals are as fab as the fashion. The beautiful and the damned haunt the South Yarra city end, and life gets a tad grungier towards St Kilda. Stop at Caffe e Cucina, where the waiters are fluent in Italian and cute too.

For factory outlets head to Bridge Road in Richmond. Start at Church Street and by the time you get to Punt Road you'll deserve your reward of this town's best cheese selection and a glass of vino at the Richmond Hill Larder.

The bohemian hub is Flinders and Brunswick streets in Fitzroy, for both new and vintage clothing. The best of the latter is at Out of the Closet, near my favourite florist, Vasette. Stop for a cuppa at Madame Sousou – you'll think you're in Paris and the locals have the same *joie de vivre!*

The arcades and graffiti-covered laneways are a credit to this city. Start at Block Arcade and weave your way to The Royal, which dates back to 1869, where you'll find Koko Black, a sinful licensed chocolate lounge. Don't miss Cathedral Arcade near Flinders Lane for Genki (cute and curious collectibles), Counter (unique crafts) and Alice Euphemia (beautiful pieces from local designers). Finish up at Miss Louise on Collins; your jaw will drop at the shoe selection, and the staff can tell a story about each princess slipper.

The first bar I was ever taken to in Melbourne was the Supper Club and I'm still a fan. Grab the lounge under the massive round window that overlooks Parliament and you'll understand its cool charm. The Wine Shop downstairs is also low on attitude and high on style. The Hotel Lindrum is central, cosy and just like Melbourne – pure style.

GETTING THERE

As a major city, you can come by road, rail or air, but when in Rome . . . in this town you've got to hop on the local trams to get around. Apart from being iconic they're efficient and for non-locals, like me, a bit of fun.

CAFFE E CUCINA
581 Chapel Street, South Yarra 3141
P: 03 9827 4139

RICHMOND HILL CAFE & LARDER
48–50 Bridge Road, Richmond 3121
P: 03 9421 2808 W: www.rhcl.com.au

OUT OF THE CLOSET
238b Flinders Street, Melbourne 3000
P: 03 9639 0980

VASETTE FLOWERS
247 Brunswick Street, Fitzroy 3065
P: 03 9419 4988 W: www.flowersvasette.com.au

MADAME SOU SOU
231 Brunswick Street, Fitzroy 3065
P: 03 9417 0400

THE BLOCK ARCADE
282–290 Collins Street, Melbourne 3000
P: 03 9654 5244

THE ROYAL ARCADE
335 Bourke Street Mall, Melbourne 3000
P: 03 9670 7777 W: www.royalarcade.com.au

CATHEDRAL ARCADE
Off Swanston Street, Melbourne 3000

MISS LOUISE
Shop 601, Grand Hyatt
123 Collins St, Melbourne 3000
P: 03 9654 7730

MELBOURNE SUPPER CLUB
Level 1, 161 Spring Street, Melbourne 3000
P: 03 9654 6300

HOTEL LINDRUM
26 Flinders Street, Melbourne 3000
P: 03 9668 1111 W: www.hotellindrum.com.au

CREATOURS
P: 03 9822 0556 W: www.creatours.com.au

SHOPPING SECRETS & HIDDEN SECRETS TOURS
P: 03 9329 9665 W: www.shoppingsecrets.com

OR VISIT: www.visitvictoria.com

MYRTLEFORD & BRIGHT

You could have heard my screams in New Zealand the day I leapt off the edge of Mount Buffalo. Hang-gliding on the back of some (now deaf) stranger, careening full pelt 1,000 metres into an abyss, was hair-raising, but geez the view was pretty. This is just one way to check out the area between Bright and Myrtleford at either end of Mount Buffalo National Park, along the Ovens Highway. While not for everyone, you should pack an outdoorsy, adventurous spirit for this trip.

Bright is the kick-off point to the Great Alpine Way, famous for its snowfields during winter. But in the warmer months it's equally good for paragliding and delicious produce, courtesy of its inhabitants' healthy European heritage. The original workers of this fertile land went on to become the owners, and now the producers, of award-winning Italian varietal wines. The Buckland Valley reminded Colin McClaren (yes, I know that's not Italian) of his favourite place in Northern Italy, so much so he decided to build an Italian-style gourmet villa. Filled with Italian furnishings, Villa Gusto is dedicated to La Dolce Vita – even the paint on the walls was shipped in for the authentic colour. Colin can advise you on where to begin your journey throughout the region – the right asparagus farm, the best local butcher for spicy salami and, of course, top of the range wine. Like a good drop, this area just gets better with age.

MY TIP

If you're driving between Sydney and Melbourne, this is a brilliant halfway point. Stay overnight and treat yourself.

GETTING THERE

Along the Ovens Highway, about a four-hour drive northeast of Melbourne, in Victoria's high country. For those that can, helicopter in, or fly to Albury-Wodonga and catch a coach up the slope.

WHAT TO DO WHEN IN THE AREA

∞ If microlighting is not your thing, try abseiling, rock climbing, caving, mountain biking or exploring the high-range trails on horseback – the views are spectacular up top.

∞ Of course, in winter skiing is all the rage – or après-skiing for some of us!

∞ There are many resorts in the area for year-round activities; try Mt Buffalo Chalet for a touch of the high life.

EAGLE SCHOOL OF MICROLIGHTING
16 Hargreaves Road, Bright 3741
P: 03 5750 1174   W: www.eagleschool.com.au

VILLA GUSTO—LA DOLCE VITA
630 Buckland Valley Road, Bright 3741
P: 03 5756 2000   W: www.villagusto.com.au

MT BUFFALO CHALET
Mt Buffalo National Park 3740
P: 03 5755 1500   W: www.mtbuffalochalet.com.au

OR VISIT: www.visitvictoria.com

PERTH

I was one of those guilty travellers who saw Perth as a springboard to all those other amazing places WA has on offer. I'd bound off the plane just itching to get to spots like the Margaret River or the Kimberley. But I now know I was not really giving any credit to all this rich city has to offer. I recently spent a few days enjoying it on a budget and returned a fan of this truly cosmopolitan town.

To start, I advise you to get a feel for the place by hopping on a wooden Perth tram. The drivers provide a commentary all the way around town, regaling stories about everything from the Burswood Casino and Kings Park to Hay Street. Is it weird to admit that I could happily spend hours on one of these tours? They do the hard work for you, it's really interesting and you sit back and chat with other travellers from all over the world.

You must also check out the Art Gallery of Western Australia, which has inspired everyone from me to the Holmes a Court family. It's modern, everchanging and you can sign up for a guided tour.

For food, the Annalakshmi restaurant on the banks of the Swan serve delicious meals with no set price – they follow the Karma principle here and you pay what you feel it's worth and the money is used to support hospitals, both international and local. Run by volunteers from all walks of life, it's worth going there just for the 360-degree views. You could also sample some fish and chips from Amberjacks on the beach down at Cottesloe.

I know many a traveller who has decided to call this place home after first sight. There are beautiful beaches lined with Norfolk pines, gorgeous weather, access to good produce, and a city that's modern and thriving. I can understand the addiction.

GETTING THERE

Fly west! Perth is our most western capital city. It's in the southwest of the state and you can also get there by driving across the Nullabor (long trip, but worth it), by coaching it, or catching the Indian Pacific train.

WHAT TO DO WHEN IN THE AREA

∞ There's everything a 21st century city can offer – you have no excuse not to enjoy.

∞ The locals are called sandgropers for a very good reasons . . . the beaches: City, Cottesloe, Floreat, Scarborough, Sorrento, Swanbourne and Trigg Island, among others.

∞ Wildflowers bloom in this state from August to November, when the fields are awash with colour.

∞ Perth is still a great jumping off spot for places like Rockingham (a chance to meet dolphins), the Swan Valley, Subiaco and the Margaret River.

∞ Facing west, Perth is a perfect romantic place to watch the sun set with that someone special and a glass of WA vino in hand.

MY TIP

Boating on the Swan is a popular pastime and you can cruise down to Fremantle or out to Rottnest Island, with the right boat of course.

PERTH TRAM COMPANY
Astons Stables, 21 Mayfair Street, West Perth 6000
P: **08 9322 2006** W: **www.perthtram.com.au**

BURSWOOD ENTERTAINMENT COMPLEX
Great Eastern Highway, Burswood 6100
P: **08 9362 7777** W: **www.burswood.com.au**

ART GALLERY OF WESTERN AUSTRALIA
Perth Cultural Centre, Cnr Roe and Beaufort St, Perth 6000
P: **08 9492 6622** W: **www.artgallery.wa.gov.au**

ANNALAKSHMI ON THE SWAN
Jetty No 4, Barrack Street, Perth 6000
P: **08 9221 3003** W: **www.annalakshmi.com.au**

AMBERJACKS
94 Marine Parade, Cottesloe 6011
P: **08 9385 0977**

OR VISIT: **www.westernaustralia.com**

PORT DOUGLAS

This place is a bit posh. I mean, c'mon, this is where Bill Clinton felt completely at ease while in Australia. Port Douglas is fast gaining a reputation as a town where celebs can just hang out and be alone. It was put on the map by one notorious mogul, Mr Christopher Skase, and ten points to him for seeing and acting on its potential. Before then it was a sleepy old fishing town on a peninsula, somewhere between Cairns and the Daintree. But Chris and Pixie fixed up the roads (well, not them personally), lined them with exotic palm trees, built the Sheraton Mirage and its marina, and basically transformed the place. Talk about a Midas touch.

Port Douglas is hugely popular among daytrippers, and why not? From Cairns it's a glorious drive along the Cook Highway, which bends around the coast, hugging the hills, overlooking the ocean. Can the sea water here really be this clear? Once you hit Port Douglas, there is the magnificent palm-lined Four Mile Beach, and loads of places to eat, drink and be merry. Oak Beach has the reputation of being the best in the area; beautiful shells line the shore after high tide.

There are all levels of accommodation to be found here as well, whether you are a backpacker or billionaire, with more hotels popping up all the time. I love The Boathouse. Where a goat track once meandered 18 luxurious apartments now sit. Do you think the goats appreciated the ocean and rainforest views? I know the hordes of tourists flowing through these days certainly do.

 MY TIP

Looking for a cheap eat? Try the deliciously named Mango Jam Cafe on Macrossan Street.

GETTING THERE

Just under an hour's drive north of Cairns, in far north Queensland, Port Douglas is accessed via the Cook Highway, which continues on to Cooktown, much further north.

WHAT TO DO WHEN IN THE AREA

∞ Catch a boat out to the glorious Barrier Reef, or do a spot of deep ocean fishing.

∞ From here you're not far from the Daintree, so explore the rainforest, and watch out for crocs!

∞ Balmy spring days are just perfect for romantic getaways.

∞ Check out that ocean from Flagstaff Hill at the end of the main street.

SHERATON MIRAGE PORT DOUGLAS
Davidson Street, Port Douglas 4871
P: **07 4099 5888** W: **www.sheraton-mirage.com**

THE BOATHOUSE
41–43 Murphy Street, Port Douglas 4871
P: **07 4099 8800** W: **www.boathouse.com.au**

OR VISIT: **www.queenslandholidays.com.au**

STANWELL TOPS

How long can the locals keep this place to themselves? I understand their desire to stay under the radar, but when the views, the water, the parks are this good and so close to Sydney . . . it must be like holding back the tide.

Stanwell Tops is the cherry on the cake, plopped on top of an escarpment and bordered by the Royal National Park, the world's second oldest national park. I've always passed Stanwell Tops by when making my way to Wollongong. My first close inspection was just after the 2001 Christmas bushfires. The national park has now grown back to its fomer glory and is a wonderful place to go hiking, camping and swimming – Garie Beach is one of my faves. I also discovered somewhere truly fantastic to stay: the immaculate Tumbling Waters Retreat.

This beautiful place was thankfully spared any fire damage from the bushfires and is going great guns today. It's first class all the way; the owners are dedicated to bringing the natural beauty of the outdoors inside. The floor-to-ceiling windows look out over the bush and beyond to the sea, and the marble bathrooms, of all things, have everyone raving. Private dining can be arranged for that special weekend, and the infinity mineral pool is also a highlight. Built in the 1930s, it's got to be one of the state's first wet-edge pools. The Lawrence Hargrave Stream flows into it and it apparently has healing properties. I have no idea why, but it sure looks fantastic and inviting.

MY TIP

The village of Stanwell Park is worth spending some time at – the galleries are good to nose about in and it's the perfect setting for afternoon tea at the local cafes.

GETTING THERE

On the edge of the Illawarra Escarpment, about an hour's drive south of Sydney or 20 minutes north of Wollongong.

WHAT TO DO WHEN IN THE AREA

∞ A must is to hang-glide from Bald Hill, which overlooks Stanwell Park.

∞ Look out for the nearby crystal swimming holes and secluded beaches – they make welcoming dipping spots.

TUMBLING WATERS RETREAT
End of Stonehaven Road, Stanwell Tops 2508
P: 02 4294 1888 W: www.tumblingwatersretreat.com

OR VISIT: www.visitnsw.com.au

WHITSUNDAYS

I was intrigued by the idea of sailing the Whitsundays. Everyone I know who's been there returns and says, 'That was the best holiday I've ever had'. With easy access – fly in, hop on your boat and out you go – and 74 islands dotted around the sapphire waters of the Coral Sea, I get it. As most of the area is World Heritage listed, it's about as pristine as it comes. You can't fish there, but who cares when the snorkelling is this good and the abundance of fish is amazing.

When it comes to the sailing bit, you'll be sweet. No licence to ride is required, but a bit of knowledge and a lot of patience is. You could be in a dinghy and be happy here, as a boatload of British backpackers, sunburnt to a crisp of course, were when they passed me as I ate my lunch on a deserted island. They thought they'd died and gone to heaven and I agreed with them. If you're after a little more luxury, though, ProSail's *Bliss* is great but my personal recommendation is Sunsail. I've worked with them all around the world and they're a sharp outfit. They've got 'bareboat' sailing, catamarans and a product called 'By the Cabin', which is five-star all the way.

Fave spots for me: Butterfly Bay, Blue Pearly Bay, Cid Harbour, Langford Reef and Nara Inlet. If there can be only one: Whitehaven, one of the best beaches in the world, is long, white and gorgeous! This holiday is totally relaxing and unpretentious; I just know you'll return like the rest of us blissed-out sailors, chiming, 'One of the best . . .'

MY TIP

Visit Mantaray Bay, Hook Island. Great snorkelling, friendly fish and, with the island as a backdrop, lovely photos.

GETTING THERE

About 1,100 km north of Brisbane, fly to Hamilton Island or Proserpine, which is 37 km to Shute Harbour, the jumping off point for the Whitsundays. From there it's smooth sailing.

WHAT TO DO WHEN IN THE AREA

∞ Don't forget to load up on books and board games.

∞ Hamilton Island has everything you need to get yourself ready – general store, chemist, even a post office – you're sorted.

∞ Travel lightly as there's not too much storage space on-board boats, and no heels on deck!

∞ Don't forget your snorkelling gear, sunscreen and hat – it can be hot out there.

SUNSAIL WHITSUNDAYS
Marina Village, Hamilton Island Marina 4803
P: 07 4948 9509 W: www.sunsailwhitsundays.com

PROSAIL WHITSUNDAYS
251 Shute Harbour Road, Airlie Beach 4802
P: 07 4946 7533 W: www.prosail.com.au

OR VISIT:www.queenslandholidays.com.au

YARRA VALLEY

Hmm, I'm not sure whether to list this as a wine tour, a gourmet safari or a drive holiday? What I do know is that this is one of the most beautiful, fertile valleys in Victoria, it's an easy drive from the city and it is consistently delivering award-winning wines, produce and accommodation. My first trip here involved a drive that took in Lilydale, Yarra Glen (great antique shopping), the valley itself (Yarra Valley Dairy has cheeses to die for), Healesville (the hotel there has wonderful food and accommodation, with double rooms that have fireplaces), and finally the lovely little town of Marysville.

I felt like I was in a car commercial when I drove between Healesville and Narbethon. It's an area called the Black Spur and the narrow road winds between towering ash trees, second in height only to Californian Redwoods; we're talking 100 metres plus. Awesome.

Maryville felt like stepping back in time. An old-fashioned sweet shop, museum, galleries and a post office shop that sells old linen and lace. Beech Forest is worth wandering through and try to see the Steavenson Falls in the evening, when it's lit by its own natural hydro-electricity display. I'm yet to take the turn off to Lake Mountain in the Yarra Ranges National Park, but I hear it has some of Australia's top cross-country ski tracks.

However you sample this neck of the woods, go with a healthy appetite and a loose schedule. There's just so much here – fertile is the word!

MY TIP

A tasty Pinot is the wine of choice to take home with you. The rich soils and cool climate here combine to deliver some of the nation's best.

GETTING THERE

About 50 km to the east of Melbourne's CBD. Drive there, or train it to Lilydale.

WHAT TO DO WHEN IN THE AREA

∞ Arrive in style: chopper in from the city in minutes to Chateau Yering, Victoria's first vineyard, and stay for a meal or a night.

∞ Visit the Healesville Sanctuary to commune with the creatures of the wild.

YARRA VALLEY VISITOR INFORMATION CENTRE
The Old Courthouse, Harker Street, Healesville 3777
P: **03 5962 2600** W: **www.visityarravalley.com.au**

YARRA VALLEY DAIRY
McMeikans Road, Yering 3770
P: **03 9739 0023** W: **www.yvd.com.au**

HEALESVILLE HOTEL
256 Maroondah Highway, Healesville 3777
P: **03 5962 4002** W: **www.healesvillehotel.com.au**

HEALESVILLE SANCTUARY
Badger Creek Road, Healesville 3777
P: **03 5957 2800** W: **www.zoo.org.au**

OR VISIT: **www.visitvictoria.com**

YOUNG

While all the statistics tell us that people are leaving country towns in droves, here's a community with a booming population. Young families (pardon the pun) are relocating back to the town, choosing to raise their children here, where they truly feel part of a community in the real sense of the word. There are business opportunities and restaurants with chefs that are actually excited about what they're creating, as well as vineyards . . . and don't forget those cherries – you've got to go home with a crate.

This town is moving forward, no doubt due to the fact that the locals are happy to contribute. For example, a group of volunteers drawn from all over the community recently got together to revamp the disused Southern Cross Hall and turn it into an arts centre and cinema. Did you know that more than 50 per cent of country towns in NSW have limited or no access to cinema or film? Young was one of those towns, but not any more.

I love the spirit of this country community and tourists can't help but pick up on that vibe. The produce is fresh and first class. You've got to sample it either at the Country Providore or Zouch – actually, try both. There's also the Chinese Gardens, and Carrington Park is great for picnics.

I was mightily impressed with this place. If you'd like to see a country town where the locals are genuinely excited by their future, head to Young.

WHAT TO DO WHEN IN THE AREA

∞ Go red at the Cherry Festival in November and December.

∞ Visit the Lambing Flat Museum for a slice of Australia's rich past.

YOUNG VISITOR INFORMATION CENTRE
2 Short Street, Young 2594
P: 02 6382 3394 W: www.visityoung.com.au

SOUTHERN CROSS CINEMA
Southern Cross Hall, Main Street, Young 2594
P: 02 6382 1000 W: www.yourmovies.com.au

LAMBING FLAT FOLK MUSEUM
Campbell Street, Young 2594
P: 02 6382 2248

THE COUNTRY PROVIDORE
143 Boorowa Street, Young 2594
P: 02 6382 7255

ZOUCH RESTAURANT/CAFE
26 Zouch Street, Young 2594
P: 02 6382 2775

OR VISIT: www.visitnsw.com.au

MY TIP

Historic Boorowa is worth a stop before you arrive in Young. The local pool is perfect on a hot day, and the beautiful main streeet has some classic country pubs.

GETTING THERE

Young is about an hour's drive from Cowra. Head along the Hume Highway via Albury, or go via Dubbo and Orange. The train also makes a whistle stop.

SUMMER

BAY OF FIRES

This adventurous, four-day walk is for those of us who love the outdoors, with a few creature comforts thrown in. A little bit of physical exertion, but nothing that will pull a muscle. I did this trip for my holidays, not work, and it goes down as one of my best adventures ever. Tasmania just doesn't disappoint. From its natural surroundings to the professional grasp the locals seem to have of tourism, with this trip, I promise you, you're signing up for an amazing experience.

The journey begins softly: a group of around ten people, a couple of capable guides, and a trek through Mount William National Park. Beautiful wildflowers, the odd wild animal, pristine bush. By the afternoon the coast is revealed. Here you are at the wild waters of Cod Bay and one long stretch of beach after another are yours to wander along in, almost, utter isolation.

When you're ready to collapse there's five-star camping and gourmet meals. I even had a bowl of warm water with witchhazel placed outside my tent, a wonderful treat and very refreshing. Sure, this is camping, but you're hardly roughing it!

While the highlight for me was the coastline, the 14 km hike to the Ken Latona-designed Bay of Fires Lodge, unveils a sight to behold. This ecologically sustainable paradise has won just about every architectural award there is. I was bowled over by the light: the floor-to-ceiling windows make it feel as though you're outside when you're in.

We indulged in three-course gourmet meals plucked straight from local providores, sang around the roaring fire at night, went kayaking during the day, and on the way home from the trip we stopped off at a local winery to toast our wonderful wilderness experience. All I can say is that, when it comes to the Bay of Fires, I loved every second of it.

GETTING THERE

Mount William National Park is on Tasmania's northeast coast. The tour starts at Evandale, near Launceston. From there you are driven to Boulder Point, where the walk begins.

WHAT TO DO WHEN IN THE AREA

∞ Check out the wildlife in the National Park: wedge-tail eagles, sea eagles, Tasmanian devils, Bennetts wallabies – too many to name.

∞ Dive, swim, snorkel or paddle on top of the waters at the beautiful beaches of Cod Bay.

∞ Explore the rocky shores and dunes.

∞ Curl up and read a book – you can be as relaxed as you wish here.

MY TIP

Spend some time in the meditation room: it looks straight out over the ocean and is warmed by the sun during the day, with an extra simple detail – no mirrors.

BAY OF FIRES WALK
P: **03 6331 2006** W: **www.bayoffires.com.au**
OR VISIT: **www.tourismtasmania.com.au**

DAYLESFORD

When you drive into Daylesford there's almost a traffic jam on the roundabouts, and don't even start me on the queues to get a coffee at my favourite cafe on the weekend. But it wasn't always like this. Some 30 years ago it was on struggle street. The glory of the gold rush days were but a memory, unemployment high, half the shopfronts closed and traditional industries struggled. Then a small group of courageous dreamers built a restaurant worthy of the journey. Of course, I'm talking about the Lake House, which has won just about every award in the business and has just opened a successful spa retreat. Travellers now beat a path to the area to sample the world-class cuisine and to luxuriate in style.

You can't visit without also popping into the Convent Gallery. I didn't know what hit me when I met dynamic owner Tina Banitska, the definition of a 'pocket rocket'. These old school grounds began life as Blarney Castle back in the 1860s, built for the gold commissioner and his family. In 1880 the Catholic Church bought it and the Holy Cross Convent for Girls rocked the halls till the 1970s. You can still feel the girls' presence as many of their rooms are intact. When Tina found the place it was in total disrepair. Again, inspiration struck and now it's jammed with seven art galleries spread over three levels. The two-and-a-half hectares of gardens set in Wombat Hill Botanical Gardens are put to good use for functions and there's a waiting list for weddings in the old school chapel. Ah, don't you just love a success story.

MY TIP

I'd travel miles to satisfy my tastebuds and I never leave Daylesford without a spicy, hot black sausage from the butcher on Vincent Street.

GETTING THERE

Set in the State's scenic central highlands, 110 km north of Melbourne, drive there via the Midland Highway.

WHAT TO DO WHEN IN THE AREA

∞ The beautiful lakes in the area, including Jubilee Lake and Lake Daylesford, are great for a bit of boating in this bucolic region.

∞ Along with Hepburn Springs, this area is regarded as spa central. So stock up on the mineral springs water—fabulous, as only water can be!

∞ Daylesford Historical Society Museum is known for its pioneer collection, including relics from the gold rush era.

∞ In December the Highland Festival gets underway, so fling away!

DAYLESFORD REGIONAL
VISITOR INFORMATION CENTRE
98 Vincent Street, Daylesford 3460
P: 03 5321 6123 W: www.visitvictoria.com

LAKE HOUSE
King Street, Daylesford 3460
P: 03 5348 3329 W: www.lakehouse.com.au

CONVENT GALLERY
Corner Hill and Daly streets, Daylesford 3460
P: 03 5348 3211 W: www.theconvent.com.au

DAYLESFORD HISTORICAL SOCIETY MUSEUM
100 Vincent Street, Daylesford 3460
P: 03 5348 1453
W: www.ddhs.goldlinksweb.com

OR VISIT: www.visitvictoria.com

EUMUNDI & SUNSHINE COAST

I first went to Eumundi about 15 years ago, when it was just a sleepy little village with some cool weekend markets. You could have heard a pin drop on Memorial Avenue. Cut to today and . . . Boom! . . . you now find (if you can make it through the hordes) one of the biggest, most successful open-air markets in the country.

It's an institution on the Sunshine Coast, and these markets are strictly controlled by the Eumundi Historical Society. They insist stallholders must be from the local region and have produced or made what they're selling. I love that concept as the result is high-quality products with original flair. There's such a variation of curios, I guarantee you can knock over your Christmas list in one hit.

I recommend Eats for coffee, but if they're really busy head for the Green Bean Cafe, the old health food store, or seek out Stan in the markets, who has the red espresso machine and has been in business for over 35 years. The Imperial Hotel has a fantastic beer garden and Joe's Waterhole is able to draw international music acts on a regular basis.

Judging by the traffic chaos of my last trip, I highly recommend you stay in town. Matter of fact, just a short stroll from the markets is Eumundi's Hidden Valley B&B (which was once called Taylors Damn Fine B&B). When you lay eyes on the view of Mount Cooroy from the wide verandah of this original Queensland homestead, I'd be surprised if you make it to the shops at all. Throw your diet out the window, too. The food is so good – the owners used to run an award-winning restaurant in Victoria's Barwon Heads – that guests have plead for a place in their private cooking classes.

Damn fine!

GETTING THERE

About 20 minutes drive from Noosa on the Sunshine Coast; a bus runs regularly to and from the markets on Saturdays and Wednesdays from Noosa Heads, Tewantin, Parklands, Cooroy and Noosaville.

WHAT TO DO WHEN IN THE AREA

∞ Shop, shop, shop til you drop!

∞ Eumundi started life as a timber and dairy town, so take a look at the buildings here, constructed between 1890 and 1920.

∞ In the heart of the Sunshine Coast, don't forget to visit all those beaches.

MY TIP

You see it, you like it, you buy it! Haggling on price is okay, but don't go in too hard – the goods here are worth the ticket price.

THE ORIGINAL EUMUNDI MARKETS
Memorial Drive, Eumundi 4567
P: 07 5442 7106 W: www.eumundimarkets.com.au

EATS AT EUMUNDI
86 Memorial Drive, Eumundi 4567
P: 07 5442 8555

JOE'S WATERHOLE HOTEL
8 Memorial Drive, Eumundi 4567
P: 07 5442 8144

EUMUNDI'S HIDDEN VALLEY
Eumundi–Noosa Road, Eumundi 4567
P: 07 5442 8685

OR VISIT: www.queenslandholidays.com.au

FORBES

Forbes' slogan is 'friendly, historic and inviting', and from my recent trip I can tick all the above. This true-blue country community welcome the new and protect their own. I went to a fundraiser at the local bowls club and was amazed at the massive turnout in 40-degree heat, and how quickly they accepted me. We had a ball, if a bit melted. Naturally, the local pool was a top spot to cool off and the children had no qualms in dunking me.

That evening I ducked into the Albion Hotel to see the tunnels underneath, which were once used to transport gold after one too many coaches were robbed by bushrangers. You see, Forbes has this fantastic gold rush history and where there's gold . . . Back in the 1850s, there were tens of thousands of prospectors setting up tents around here. The Albion was just one of many pubs that sold more alcohol than anywhere else in Australia. Of course, the odd bushranger also wanted to get in on the act, and their exploits are now folklore: Ben Hall, Frank Gardiner, Johnnie Gilbert and their wicked little gangs. Apparently, Hall, who is buried in Forbes alongside Ned Kelly's sister Kate, was dashingly handsome, flash and a fine horseman – ah, why do we always fall for the bad ones?

Today, Forbes is a flourishing rural town, so do make an effort to see the state's flashest sale yards and the southern hemisphere's biggest dairy. A real treat would be a stay at Burrawang West Station – wow! It's the outback's most luxurious homestead: 4,000 hectares of rich pasture land overlooking the Lachlan River. This property has been loved by so many – no doubt for its breathtaking natural beauty – and while the owners may have experienced bursts and busts, the earth continues to deliver. Burrawang is now home to first class accommodation, an amazing art collection and as many activities as you could hope for. I'd like to say it's a resort but it's also a successful beef station with just as many tales to tell as the town itself.

GETTING THERE

It's about a five-and-half-hour drive west of Sydney, in the Lachlan Valley. Also serviced by coaches and trains.

MY TIP

So many country towns pull down and revamp their street fronts, but here's a community who valiantly protect theirs. A Heritge Trail has been mapped to share all the juicy stories – contact the tourism information centre for details.

WHAT TO DO WHEN IN THE AREA

∞ Bail up! Do the bushranger thing and visit Ben Hall's grave (the cemetery is National Trust listed) and the Bushrangers Hall of Fame Museum in the Albion Hotel.

∞ There are a few good wineries – who knew – try them.

∞ Visit Lake Forbes (where you can waterski at the Aquatic Centre) and the Lachlan River to appreciate the inland waterways.

FORBES VISITOR INFORMATION CENTRE
Railway Station, Union Street, Forbes 2871
P: 02 6852 4155 W: www.visitnsw.com.au

ALBION HOTEL (and Bushrangers Hall of Fame)
135 Lachlan Street, Forbes 2871
P: 02 6851 1881

BURRAWANG WEST STATION
Ootha 2875
P: 02 6897 5277 W: www.burrawangwest.com.au

OR VISIT: www.visitnsw.com.au

FRENCH ISLAND

Even the locals refer to French Island as 'the forgotten island'. And I must admit, before I went there to do a story I'd never heard of it, yet it's so amazingly central to everything. From the island you can see the Mornington Peninsula, across to Phillip Island and out to the Strzelecki Ranges – it's a brilliant holiday base. Perhaps this is why Kylie Minogue chose to buy a holiday home here. Or perhaps it's the isolation – it might be near everything but the only way ashore is via a ferry. But don't worry, it's just a 30-minute ride.

Once you're there, you'll find a large country wilderness area, awesome ocean views and more koalas than I've ever seen in my life. In fact they outnumber the locals 50 to 1. There are so many they have to relocate around 200 each year to the mainland as they literally eat themselves out of house and home.

I think French Island is a wonderful place for children; not too many tourists and loads to do. A fun way to see the island is to sign up for a Llama Tour. Can you believe it? Two enterprising locals thought, 'Why not bring a bunch of llamas over to the hobby farm?' From there, they progressed to loading them up with a gourmet picnic and letting all-comers take a wander! I had such a peaceful day out on this trip. The llamas don't have an attitude at all (unlike some horses I know) so you really bond with your four-legged friend by day's end. You get a fantastic tour of the countryside and a great lunch to boot.

The residents of French Island have to generate their own power so there's no 'street' lighting as such. So if you're off for an evening beach stroll, don't forget that torch.

GETTING THERE

The ferry leaves from Stony Point on Mornington Peninsula and Cowes on Phillip Island; both south of Melbourne.

WHAT TO DO WHEN IN THE AREA

∞ The people here love to host school groups, so get a team together; perhaps even for a murder mystery weekend for the adults.

∞ A spot of fishing, bushwalking, swimming and bike riding are all on the agenda.

∞ If you're visiting, think as the islanders do: ecologically. There are eco tours and and an Eco Farm to indulge in.

∞ Seventy per cent of the island is a national park, and it also has the French Island Marine National Park, a wonderful area to explore the mudflats, seagrass and salt marshes.

FRENCH ISLAND LLAMA EXPERIENCE
Tanderum, Tenchain Road, French Island 3921
P: 03 5980 1287 W: www.fillamas.com.au

FRENCH ISLAND ECO TOURS
Lot 1, Tankerton Road, French Island 3920
P: 1300 307 054 W: www.frenchislandecotours.com.au

MCLEOD ECO FARM
McLeod Road, French Island 3921
P: 03 5980 1224 W: www.mcleodecofarm.com

FRENCH ISLAND GENERAL STORE
Tankerton Road, French Island 3920
P: 03 5980 1209

OR VISIT: www.visitvictoria.com

GLENWORTH VALLEY

Okay, here's one for the horse nuts . . . me included. It can send you crazy living in a city with few options for a good bolt. Solution for Sydneysiders: Glenworth Valley. Whether you ride or not, this heavenly patch of land answers many prayers. Turn off the freeway and you'll find your shoulders instantly relax once you spy the lush bushland as you creep down the mountain to the valley. Then the excitement really starts to build and, sure enough, when the centre does reveal itself, it does not disappoint. Laid out in front of you are three and a half thousand acres of splendid Aussie wilderness.

With regards to riding, I don't like going to places where they muster you into a line, fast up front, slow pokes down back, and don't get that order muddled. At Glenworth they spend time establishing your level of skill, choosing the right horse for you and kitting you with safety equipment. And here's the good bit: they let you out on your own, free range! They do also offer guide-led tours and there are experts along the trails to look after you, but they encourage you to go it alone if you can get yourself going in a confident and safe manner. They want you to make the most of it.

There are masses of wildlife and several trails – through rainforest, along Poplan Creek (my favourite), past Aboriginal rock paintings and by rock pools. Word is, the latter spot is so hot that a growing number of wedding proposals are happening here. Best of all, they can even come back for the wedding.

WHAT TO DO WHEN IN THE AREA

∞ This is a real multi-fun venue; you can also abseil, kayak, bushwalk, ride quad bikes and duel in laser squirmish (whoa!).

∞ Ask them about the two-day cattle muster that can be organised for groups.

∞ If you want more than a day out of the city, you can camp on site, and even hire a tent if you need one. They also cater for camper trailers but there is no power, so bring a generator.

∞ Enjoy a picnic or barbeque beside the creek during your lunch break.

∞ Putting on a conference, wedding, photo shoot, launch or other function? No problems, Glenworth to the rescue.

MY TIP

Glenworth plays host to several festivals throughout the year, the most popular being the annual Peats Ridge Music Festival in December – a three-day event celebrating world music and sustainable living that features over 100 acts.

GETTING THERE

It's just over an hour's drive north from Sydney Harbour Bridge, depending on the traffic heading out of town.

GLENWORTH VALLEY HORSE RIDING
69 Cooks Road, Peats Ridge 2250
P: 02 4375 1222 W: www.glenworth.com.au

PEATS RIDGE SUSTAINABLE ARTS & MUSIC FESTIVAL
W: www.peatsridgefestival.com.au

OR VISIT: www.visitnsw.com.au

Wilderness Trail 2hr - 11km

Rainforest Trail 2-3hr - 13km >

Rockpools Trail 2hr - 10km >

< Popran Creek Trail 2hr - 8km

GOLD COAST & HINTERLAND

I know most travellers love the Gold Coast for all its glitz and glamour; after all, that is what the place is famous for. But my favourite spots in this area are to be found in the hinterland. Lush tropical rainforest, cosy mountain villages, waterfalls – the pace is laidback and the locals all seem to have a glow about them. Think Tamborine Mountains, Ferny Glen, Mudgeeraba, Binna Burra . . . perfect antidotes to the hustle and bustle of the seaside resorts when you need a break. Lots of places to quietly wander and reflect.

Another way to achieve that Hinterland glow, quick sticks, is to visit Camp Eden, a health playground for grown-ups. If the idea of a health camp sends shivers down your spine you're not alone, but I loved it here. You rise at dawn for a bit of yoga in the fresh air, then go for either a run or walk through the most beautiful bushland. A huge, healthy brekkie awaits you and then the day is yours to either relax, be pampered or challenge yourself to all sorts of activities, from tennis and abseiling to a flying fox and the scariest ropes course in the country. Go on . . . I dare you to complete the entire challenge!

Of course, the Gold Coast area is also fantastic for young ones – and that would be all of us, wouldn't it? There are all those Worlds: Movie World, Wet 'n' Wild Water World, Dreamworld, Sea World; and those beaches. It's enough to tire the littlies (and biggies) out!

You could also cruise to Morton Island or feed the birds, Mary Poppins style, at the Currumbin Wildlife Sanctuary. There are also loads of extreme aerial and water sports to get your heart thumping.

Just too much to do and never enough time!

GETTING THERE

The Gold Coast is easy to get to. It's around an hour's drive southeast of Brisbane; there's an international airport, heaps of buses and tour coaches and the train stops there. Camp Eden is about 30 minutes from the Gold Coast.

WHAT TO DO WHEN IN THE AREA

∞ When in Rome . . . well, the Gold Coast . . . you just must visit Jupiters Casino – it reeks glitz and glamour, with great Moulin Rouge-style shows.

∞ For speed, try the Aquaduck tours; it travels on land and water.

∞ Or if you want an aerial escapade, take a flight in a Tiger Moth, complete with Biggles-style helmet and goggles.

MY TIP

If you book into Camp Eden and you love your chocs, carbs or ciggies, ease off them at least a week or two before you arrive; they are definitely on the no-no list and the withdrawal headaches just aren't worth it.

HELLO GOLD COAST
W: www.hellogoldcoast.com.au/attractions.html

CAMP EDEN HEALTH RETREAT
Currumbin Creek Road, Currumbin Valley 4223
P: 07 5533 0333 W: www.campeden.com.au

CONRAD JUPITERS
Broadbeach Island, Gold Coast 4218
P: 07 5592 8100 W: www.conrad.com.au/jupiters

OR VISIT: www.queenslandholidays.com.au

HOBART

Spend a moment at Salamanca Place and you'll understand why backpackers from home and abroad are beating a path to this city. The hip vibe is an added bonus to Tasmania's natural beauty. Salamanca Markets come alive on the weekend but there's heaps of nearby places to meet like-minded souls.

Keep a look out for Club Salsa, where around 250 people do their darndest to keep up with Gaia, the stunning South American teacher. Follow that with a visit to one of Hobart's oldest and most popular pubs, Knopwoods Retreat, for a warm Gluhwein. It's quite ironic that 'Noppies' was once a brothel; these days it still shares the love but brings flirty folk together legally. The Republic Bar has great live music but I couldn't get enough of the jazz/folk band sending the crowd into a spin at The Salamanca Arts Centre.

The city bursts at the seams during the Sydney to Hobart Yacht Race, so get in early for accommodation. If you're on a budget, try The Pickled Frog, Hobart's best hostel. For your laundry, head down to the Machine Laundry Cafe; it's got all the washing facilities plus a delicious cafe serving brekkie all day – even a dog-a-chino for pooch.

The hippest hotel has to be The Henry Jones Art Hotel. Set in the old IXL jam factory, it creates a market for students of the Tasmanian School of Art. They sell their work in the hotel, alongside more established local artists. Like Hobart, the work, the mood, the talent is ever-happening.

MY TIP

To sample Tassie's great seafoods try Fish Frenzy. There's normally a queue going down Elizabeth Street Pier to get in, but it's worth the big paper cone your dinner is served in.

GETTING THERE

This state capital is in the south of Tasmania, and it's easy to get to. Hop on a plane or catch the ferry if you're out of state. Or drive, bike, train or bus in if you're already there.

WHAT TO DO WHEN IN THE AREA

∞ Ahoy! Catch all the excitement as the Rolex Sydney to Hobart Yacht Race finishes sometime before the New Year.

∞ Spin the wheel at Australia's first casino, Wrest Point, beautifully located on the river front.

∞ Climb the heights of Mt Wellington for a stunning view of the city and Derwent River.

∞ The historic Port Arthur is nearby, so pay homage to its haunting past.

∞ Explore the Derwent River. This fabulous waterway runs from New Norfolk in the north to its mouth at Hobart. You can hop on a ferry or cruise or even cycle along its foreshore.

CLUB SALSA AT THE VENUE
8 Salamanca Place, Hobart 7000
P: 0418 595 520

KNOPWOODS RETREAT
39 Salamanca Place, Hobart 7000
P: 03 6223 5808

REPUBLIC BAR AND CAFE
299 Elizabeth Street, Hobart 7000
P: 03 6234 6954 W: www.republicbar.com

SALAMANCA ARTS CENTRE
77 Salamanca Place, Hobart 7000
P: 03 6234 8414 W: www.salarts.org.au

THE PICKLED FROG
281 Liverpool Street, Hobart 7000
P: 03 6234 7977

MACHINE LAUNDRY CAFE
12 Salamanca Square, Battery Point 7004
P: 03 6224 9922 W: www.machinelaundrycafe.com.au

HENRY JONES ART HOTEL
25 Hunter Street, Hobart 7000
P: 03 6231 6391 W: www.thehenryjones.com

FISH FRENZY
Elizabeth Street Pier, Hobart 7000
P: 03 6231 2134 W: www.fishfrenzy.com.au

OR VISIT: www.discovertasmania.com.au

KANGAROO ISLAND

There is so much to do and see here you'll barely have time to check out the island's namesake. It is incredibly close to Adelaide but still quite rural. There is virtually no mobile range and the atmosphere is totally laidback. Maybe that's why the health retreats and B&Bs seem to do so well here. It's definitely a place to get away and completely chill.

A 4WD is the best way to get around to check the legendary rock formations, the Remarkable Rocks and Admirals Arch. Head to Kirkpatrick Point within the Flinders Chase National Park for the dramatic cluster of granite boulders that date back 500 million years.

Then there's the marine life. This is our third largest island, with over 500 km of mainly undeveloped coastline, so you can imagine how amazing the diving is. Fishing, boating, surfing and spearfishing are all top-drawer, although keep an eye out for the odd unwanted fin, no doubt lured by the large colonies of sea lions.

The wildlife is incredible. There are 26 parks and reserves on the island, so nature runs wild here. The locals are proud of the fact that the island is fox and rabbit free, and no predators equals flourishing wildlife. You can get close to the sea lions at Seal Bay and there are also echidnas, wallabies, goannas and all sorts of birds to spot. Here's an interesting fact: the island's poultry is in hot demand by chefs the world over because the chooks roam free. By the time they make it to the dinner plate they're big, chunky and mighty tasty!

WHAT TO DO WHEN IN THE AREA

∞ Savour the local produce; it's highly acclaimed: cheeses, honey, olive oil and fresh seafood, including lobster straight from the ocean. The yoghurt is famous – I could take a crate of it home!

∞ See the little penguins do a nightly walk to their burrows near Kingscote.

∞ Not one, not two, but three lighthouses are open for inspection.

MY TIP

Visit the sea lions with a local guide – it will then be nice and safe as even the baby seals may get overly curious of you.

GETTING THERE

Just 16 km off the Fleurieu Peninsula (or 120 km southwest of Adelaide), Kangaroo Island is just a ferry ride from Cape Jervis or a short plane trip from Adelaide.

KANGAROO ISLAND GATEWAY VISITOR INFORMATION CENTRE
Howard Drive, Penneshaw 5222
P: 08 8553 1185 W: www.tourkangarooisland.com.au

KANGAROO ISLAND DIVING SAFARIS
RSD 451, Kingscote 5223
P: 08 8559 3225 W: www.kidivingsafaris.com

KANGAROO ISLAND WILDERNESS TOURS
42 Cook Street, Parndana 5220
P: 08 8559 5033 W: www.wildernesstours.com.au

OR VISIT: www.southaustralia.com

LAUNCESTON

Maybe because Tassie's third-oldest city is also a university town, there is a youthful energy here. Every time I visit, the locals are buzzing about their business and life seems to be lived outdoors, making the most of this wondrous environment. While travellers once breezed through to other adventures, 'Lonnie' has now become the destination. Little wonder with so many great things to do.

Dining out is a real treat with the development of the Old Seaport wharf on the Tamar. All sorts of new and wonderful eateries and wine bars have opened up. After dining, enjoy a walk along the marina – it's quite romantic.

Cataract Gorge is another highlight. It's a great area to explore on foot. Boag's Brewery has one of my all-time favourite behind-the-scenes tours. You can check out the skill that produces this fine amber liquid and tell the team I said 'hello' – they look tough but they're absolute softies. The Tamar Valley is home to many fine vineyards, so go ahead and try them. Lonnie is also home to Tasmania's first five-star B&B, Hatherley House. This to-die-for mansion is all modern inside but French colonial outside. The garden is sublime and the whole site is registered with the National Trust.

Lonnie is just so laid back and cruisy these days with loads of personality to hold your attention.

MY TIP

Did you know that Tassie is divided into two beer drinking turfs – Boags in the north and Cascade in the south? It's social suicide if you ask for the wrong one at a local watering hole. I'll just stick with the vino, me thinks.

GETTING THERE

In the north of the state, Launceston is neatly sited on the juncture of the Tamar, North Esk and South Esk rivers. Drive in on the Midlands or Bass highways, or arrive via the scenic Tasman Highway. You can also fly or train in.

WHAT TO DO WHEN IN THE AREA

∞ Take a lift on Launceston's Basin Chairlift, the longest single chairlift span in the world; the views are spectacular.

∞ You have to see Penny Royal World – it's quite something.

∞ The popular Evandale Market is on every Sunday, selling heaps of goods, including local produce.

∞ The Aquarius Roman Baths are great mineral baths; go on, immerse yourself in luxury.

OLD LAUNCESTON SEAPORT
Seaport Boulevard, Old Launceston 7250
W: www.oldlauncestonseaport.com

J. BOAG & SON
21 Shields Street, Launceston 7250
P: 03 6332 6332 W: www.boags.com.au

HATHERLEY HOUSE
43 High Street, Launceston 7250
P: 03 6334 7727 W: www.hatherleyhouse.com.au

PENNY ROYAL WORLD
147 Paterson Street, Launceston 7250
P: 03 6334 3975 W: www.pennyroyalworld.com.au

EVANDALE MARKET
Falls Park, Logan Road, Evandale 7212
P: 03 6391 8900/0418 134 511

AQUARIUS ROMAN BATHS
127–133 George Street, Launceston 7250
P: 03 6331 2255 W: www.romanbath.com.au

OR VISIT: www.discovertasmania.com.au

MALDON

If I say, that visiting Maldon is like stepping back in time, not only would that put you to sleep, it's not quite true. This is a National Trust town with a glorious past, but the locals are excited by their future: the population's growing, there's a spring in people's steps and the town's absolutely buzzing. I wonder if this was the same mood here back in 1853, the height of the heady goldrush age when some 20,000 prospectors flocked to Maldon. Sadly, when the gold ran out so did the population, dropping to under 2,000. But their chattels make for great trade today, with fabulous antique shopping and loads more bygone-era attractions.

For fab views of the town and surrounding area, head to the lookouts at Mount Tarrengower and Anzac Hill. If you're there on one of the days Rosie and Bubbles canter into town pulling their stagecoach, you can tour the town in style. Or pick up a guide from the information centre. The Maldon Lolly Shop will send your dentist into a spin, and buy up big at Lavender and Lace and the old general store that now houses Grainstore Antiques. Head to the McArthurs for afternoon tea; the fluffy scones are award-winners and the recipe a closely guarded secret. But the big thing to do is to arrive in Maldon by the Victorian Goldfields Railway. You steam in from Castlemaine, winding through the forest and countryside, and you can learn how to drive the old steam locomotive. It's a credit to the volunteers . . . and magnificent Maldon.

MY TIP

This is a real heritage town, voted Australia's First Notable Town in the mid 1960s. So do the heritage thing and learn about Maldon's rich history. You'll be surprised.

GETTING THERE

A two-hour drive from Melbourne; 15 mins from Castlemaine, but catch the train. The journey is part of the fun.

WHAT TO DO WHEN IN THE AREA

∞ A city that loves to celebrate. Don't forget to check out 'Maldon in Winter', a two-week celebration with literary lunches, roaring log fires, hot roasts, long walks and clear starry nights.

∞ In early November the town comes alive with the Maldon Folk Festival.

∞ Take a tour of a real gold mine: Carman's Tunnel.

∞ Some great wineries nearby include Grange Hill and Chapple's Cairn.

MALDON VISITOR INFORMATION CENTRE
P: 03 5475 2569

MALDON LOLLY SHOP
20 High Street, Maldon 3463
P: 03 5475 1136

LAVENDER AND LACE LIVING
High Street, Maldon 3463
P: 03 5475 1075/03 5475 2357

MCARTHUR'S RESTAURANT
43 Main Street, Maldon 3463
P: 03 5475 1094

OLD GRAINSTORE ANTIQUES
Corner Templeton and Edwards streets, Maldon 3463
P: 03 5475 2902

VICTORIAN GOLDFIELDS RAILWAY
Maldon Train Station, Hornsby Street, Maldon 3463
P: 03 5475 1451 W: www.vgr.com.au

CARMAN'S TUNNEL
Parkins Reef Road, Maldon 3463
P: 03 5475 2667

OR VISIT: www.visitvictoria.com

MARGARET RIVER

'So, you like wine?' asked the car rental lady at the airport.

'Mmm, yes.'

'Good, 'coz you're going to the best place for it.'

You have to admit, this region has an embarrassment of riches. Rock star beaches, world-famous wineries, local produce that has chefs beating a path to its restaurant doors, and abundant bushland where the energy force is so strong it'll knock you off your feet. Some go for the wine, others for the surf, but I was lured by the promise of 'soulful travel', a healing retreat known as Moondance Lodge.

It proved to be one of the most serendipitous travel experiences I've ever had. Moondance promises to nourish the spirit, to let time and space collapse and to allow you to revel in nature in five-star surroundings. A big call, I know, but it's true. Even as I turned off the main winery road as a stressed city mess, I felt my body relax. The treats just kept on coming: great food, spot-on service, wonderful lodgings, and everything a body could need to be pampered.

In summer, the harvest is on in the region, the ocean has had time to warm up, the sunsets are long and the stars bright. There's an incredible feeling of abundance in the air. Visit a pristine beach within five minutes, spot dolphins, sample a winery for lunch then take a long nap on the private deck. The energy on the property is so amazing, your spirit will soar and you'll leave completely re-energised.

MY TIP

In keeping with the region, sample the Grape Healing Therapy at Moondance – the only spa treatment of its kind in Oz. The Shiraz Salt Scrub will leave your skin absolutely glowing and radiant.

GETTING THERE

This beautiful region in the southwest corner of the state is just 272 km south of Perth (a three-hour drive).

WHAT TO DO WHEN IN THE AREA

∞ Surf's up. Get going with the Yallingup Surf School – anyone can join.

∞ The Yallingup Shearing Shed guarantees a quintessential Aussie experience.

∞ Vasse Felix, not just for the wine; they have terrific art exhibitions.

∞ Gunyulgup galleries showcases the best local art.

MARGARET RIVER VISITORS CENTRE
100 Bussell Highway, Margaret River 6285
P: 08 9757 2911 W: www.margaretriver.com

MOONDANCE LODGE
Spencer Road (off Caves Road), Yallingup 6282
P: 08 9750 1777 W: www.moondancelodge.com

YALLINGUP SURF SCHOOL
PO Box 32, Yallingup 6284
P: 08 9755 2755 W: www.yallingupsurfschool.com

YALLINGUP SHEARING SHED
Lot 963, Wildwood Road, Yallingup 6282
P: 08 9655 2309

VASSE FELIX
Cnr Caves Road and Harmans Road South, Cowaramup 6282
P: 08 9756 6284 W: www.vassefelix.com.au

GUNYULGUP GALLERIES
Gunyulgup Valley Drive, Yallingup 6282
P: 08 9755 2177

OR VISIT: www.westernaustralia.com

METUNG

Metung might be a small village of only about 500 people but it's somewhere I return to constantly because there's so much to do. Once you turn off the busy Princes Highway and journey alongside the Tambo River, the sweep of Bancroft Bay opens up before you. It's these blue waters you won't want to leave and what life in the area revolves around.

This coastal town's name is an Aboriginal word that could mean either 'mainland' or 'ti-tree river bend', after the trees that line the beaches. I guess 'mainland' because it is at the eastern end of the biggest lake system in Australia – the Gippslands. Metung is mainly a boating or fishing village but I've also been parasailing to get my adrenalin going; sailed on yachts to bays and beaches that make you wonder if anyone else has ever explored them; kayaked through tiny waterways and had dolphins dance in front of me. But life here isn't entirely spent on the water; there are food trails, wineries and a cooking school that's got everyone raving.

It goes without saying that an area this beautiful inspires creativity. You'll be surprised by the amount of galleries and craft outlets. I love silversmith Hendrik Forster's work, found in nearby Nungurner. He's so good he was commissioned to make the gift from the Australian Government for Charles and Diana's wedding. For a great meal, head to the Metung Pub, a treasured spot on the waterfront, full of local characters. Environmental controls keep Metung small and quiet; locals and devoted holidaymakers wouldn't have it any other way.

MY TIP

Metung has a Farmers' Market every month on the village green and the jetty is directly in front of the site, so cruise on in by boat.

GETTING THERE

Nestled on Lake King, Metung is about 310 km from Melbourne, set in the heart of Gippsland Lakes.

WHAT TO DO WHEN IN THE AREA

∞ The waterways here come alive in summer, when the Metung Regatta sets sail in January.

∞ You definitely need to explore the Gippsland Lakes – coastal lagoons formed by a long sandy spit known as Ninety Mile Beach.

∞ Legend Rock by the shore of Bancroft Bay in Metung is part of an Aboriginal cultural trail called Bataluk, which extends from Sale in the east through Bairnsdale, Metung and Orbost to Cape Conran. It predominantly follows the Koorie trading routes of pre-colonial days. Well worth investigating.

∞ Hire a bike and pedal the East Gippsland Rail Trail that passes through villages beyond the lakes.

METUNG VISITOR INFORMATION CENTRE
Shop 3, 50 Metung Road, Metung 3904
P: 03 5156 2969 W: www.metungtourism.com.au

CULINAIRE COOKING SCHOOL
51 Cunningham Court, Swan Reach 3903
P: 03 5156 4091 W: www.culinaire-cookingschool.com.au

NUNGURNER ART GALLERY
111 Jetty Road, Nungurner 3909
P: 03 5156 3273

BATALUK CULTURAL TRAIL
W: www.gippslandinfo.com.au/Aboriginal

EAST GIPPSLAND RAIL TRAIL
W: www.eastgippslandrailtrail.com

OR VISIT: **www.visitvictoria.com**

MORNINGTON PENINSULA

For generations Victorians have treasured the drive along here, and credit must go to the railway for really opening up the area in 1889. Mornington is the main town on the peninsula and there's plenty of great beachside villages to visit as well as hinterland hamlets, not to forget the wineries, galleries, gardens and eateries – a full-on feast of things to do.

Heronswood, a beautiful historic property in Dromana, is home to Australia's largest gardening club. Wander through two hectares of formal gardens and then buy rare seedlings from them before you go. Dromana also has a caravan park with one of the best locations in the state, right on the beach. From here, head to the mountains for fabulous bushwalks.

Rye has a beautiful beach and is home to sand-sculpting. I'm not talking your average castle here; try 2,000 tonnes of sand used to create scenes from favourite Disney films. Children love it and adults can't believe that only water is added. The Rye Hotel is a popular waterhole and I love the Winelounge. They serve delicious food and carry more than 170 varieties of wines. In fact, you'll be spoilt for choice with wine on the peninsula. At Montalto Vineyard take a squiz at the growing sculpture collection in the garden. You can picnic here under the towering gums, with views out to the ocean, and staff will even point out the lucky spot where marriage proposals are often made. Is it your turn?

MY TIP

There's a great kiosk at Schnapper Point, which locals and travellers flock to for the views and the tucker.

GETTING THERE

The Mornington Peninsula forms the eastern arm of Port Phillip Bay and it's only about an hour's drive from Melbourne. You can also catch the train or bus.

WHAT TO DO WHEN IN THE AREA

∞ With over 50 cellar doors open, wine tasting is a must.

∞ Those well-shot, brightly-coloured beach huts line the beach of Port Phillip Bay. Start counting.

∞ Wednesday, in Main Street, Mornington, is market day.

∞ For those who need to satisify their swing addiction, there are 18 golf courses to choose from.

MORNINGTON PENINSULA TOURISM & VISITOR
INFORMATION CENTRE
Point Nepean Road, Dromana 3936
P: 03 5987 3078   W: www.visitmorningtonpeninsula.org

HERONSWOOD
105 Latrobe Parade, Dromana 3936
P: 03 5987 1877   W: www.thediggersclub.com.au

KANGERONG HOLIDAY PARK
105 Point Nepean Road, Dromana 3936
P: 03 5987 2080   W: www.kangerong.com.au

RYE HOTEL
2415 Point Nepean Road, Rye 3941
P: 03 5985 2277   W: www.ryehotel.com.au

WINELOUNGE
2253 Point Nepean Road, Rye 3941
P: 03 5985 8355   W: www.winelounge.com.au

MONTALTO VINEYARD & OLIVE GROVE
33 Shoreham Road, Red Hill South 3937
P: 03 5989 8412   W: www.montalto.com.au

OR VISIT: www.visitvictoria.com

NORTH COAST SURF SCHOOL

Whether you have always wanted to learn to surf, you know someone who does, or you just love hanging out with a bunch of like-minded souls, I have the surfing safari for you. Nat, Dan and Kim are three dudes living every waxhead's dream. They've all thrown in their labourers' jobs and turned their passion for surfing into a vocation – Mojosurf. Since we first met, back in 1999, business is pumping! Surely this has to be the job of a lifetime.

Essentially, if you take their five-day adventure, you hitch a ride on their bus leaving Sydney and spend the week learning to surf and wave-hopping the coast all the way north to Byron. Along the way you get to sample some of the best beaches on offer. When the surf's up, you're out there. At night there are purpose-built campsites to relax in, and that's when the fun continues.

I can't tell you how much I laughed doing this trip. We'd sing around the campfire at night, go to beaches that were crowd-free during the day, and I actually rode waves with dolphins swimming alongside me. The coastline is fully sick. The boys take you to the secret spots their parents took them to as nippers, like Crescent Head and Big Hill (not so secret now!). They also cruise up the coast to a little-known area they call Spot X (that will remain a secret), where I caught the wave of my life.

The home stretch of the trip is the surfing mecca of Byron, where you'll party like there's no tomorrow and be licking the tubes with the best of them.

Basically the trip is a wonderful excuse to combine sightseeing while learning this totally addicitive sport. The boys offer weekend and one-day excursions as well.

GETTING THERE

Pick-up points for the Mojo bus are outside the Museum of Contemporary Art in The Rocks, Sydney; Westfield in Tuggerah, and Hexham Train Station in Newcastle. The bus terminal in Byron Bay is the drop-off point.

WHAT TO DO WHEN IN THE AREA

∞ Surf, surf, and surf!

∞ Oh, boogie boarding is okay too.

∞ Bring plenty of jokes for those campfire nights, as well as a big appetite, towels, sleeping bags, hat and sunscreen, torch, camera and party funds.

∞ Don't even think about sleeping.

MY TIP

When you're in Byron ask the Mojo boys about their Byron Threesome offer – skydiving, snorkelling and surfing – all in one day, or at your leisure.

MOJOSURF AUSTRALIA
2/65 Centennial Circuit, Byron Bay 2481
P: 1800 113 044/02 6639 5100 W: www.mojosurf.com

DOLPHIN KAYAKING
P: 02 6685 8044 W: www.dolphinkayaking.com.au

OR VISIT: www.visitnsw.com.au

ORANGE

Talk about ripe, Orange is the fruit basket capital. Have you ever eaten an apple straight from an orchard tree? It's the best, like a meal in itself. Overflowing with produce, this area is where people from the city, who mainly buy their food from supermarkets, come to see and taste the real deal. I joined Maeve O'Mara's Gourmet Safari, which gave me the chance to chat to the talent behind Orange's tasty treats.

I sampled the work of Borry Gatrell at Borrodell on the Mount, a luxurious hideaway surrounded by fertile vineyards and orchards. Borry became nostalgic for apples with different tastes and flavours and planted hundreds of varieties of heritage apples. I loved his Lady of the Snow. A cute guy (Tim Hanson), who produces venison for the world's top restaurants, gave us cooking classes. The most talented chef in the area (Michael Manners of Selkirk's) took us truffle hunting then whipped up a magnificent dinner for us. The winemakers at Bloodwood, Rhonda and Stephen Doyle, loved telling us the stories behind their wines, which have names like 'Big Men In Tights', which has apparently been responsible for several pregnancies and is loved by wrestler's grandmothers. Book ahead for a bit of their vino sampling.

The Black Sheep Inn, the funkiest accommodation in town, is a great place to lay your head – you sleep where sheep were once shorn in this sympathetically restored old shed. With loads of festivals year-round, join in, take a seat at the table and sample the bounty of Orange's varied harvests.

MY TIP

You don't have to visit Borry's to buy his apples as you can order from the website and a crate will be delivered to your door, fresh and in season.

GETTING THERE

Orange is 250 km west of Sydney; it'll take about three and a half hours to drive. You can also fly in, and bus or train it.

WHAT TO DO WHEN IN THE AREA

∞ If you're not peckish (heaven knows, I always am), then visit the Orange Regional Gallery to satisfy the culture vulture within.

∞ There are over 20 vineyards in the region, a good reason to leave the car at home.

∞ Water sports, picnics, barbeques and bushwalking are for the taking at Lake Canobolas at the foot of Mount Canobolas.

GOURMET SAFARIS
P: 02 9960 5675 W: www.gourmetsafaris.com.au

BORRODELL ON THE MOUNT
Lake Canobolas Road, Orange 2800
P: 02 6465 3425 W: www.borrodell.com.au

MANDAGERY CREEK FARMED VENISON
Rocklands, Greening Lane, Orange 2800
P: 02 6365 6171 W: www.mandagerycreek.com.au

SELKIRK'S RESTAURANT
179 Anson Street, Orange 2800
P: 02 6261 1179

BLOODWOOD ESTATE
Griffin Road, Orange 2800
P: 02 6362 5631 W: www.bloodwood.com.au

BED OF ROSES & THE BLACK SHEEP INN
Forbes Road, Kyalla Park, Orange 2800
P: 02 6362 6946 W: www.bedofroses.net.au

ORANGE REGIONAL GALLERY
Byng and Peisley streets, Orange 2800
P: 02 6393 8136 W: www.org.nsw.gov.au

OR VISIT: www.visitnsw.com.au

Restricted
Area
Authorised
Persons only

ORION, CRUISE

It takes a lot for me to recommend a cruise, and I've sampled them all: the world's biggest, the most expensive, the oldest, the wildest, etc. The *Orion* is different. It's definitely five-star luxury, but because it's not trying to win any 'size' awards, it's intimate enough to take you to the more out-of-the-way places along its route. You get to experience comfort and exploration in one.

This was the first liner to visit East Timor after independence, and they also cruise to Papua New Guinea, Antarctica, the Kimberley and more. But the trip I loved so much that I then sent my parents on it, is the one that circumnavigates Tasmania. Before *Orion*, travelling to some of the locations they visited on the Apple Isle seemed too hard for my parents, but they agreed to this Christmas pressie from me and returned raving.

The breathtaking beauty of Tasmania, a land of such dramatic coastlines and rugged mountains, can be appreciated in a whole new way from the sea angle. *Orion* has the ability to visit places you would normally only access after days of arduous trekking, as well as the tried-and-true crowd pleasers. Wine Glass Bay was one such hit. You can step ashore via a small landing boat and learn more about the area from a local guide, who will take you on a hike across to Coles Bay. Some fellow passengers took a joy flight to get an aerial view; others ventured on a gourmet tour. Everyone departed the area happy and with a greater understanding of the Freycinet.

The stop at King Island put the foodies in a spin but everyone raved about the food on board as well as the menus, which were designed by uber-chef Serge Dansereau using fantastic local produce. This trip is loved by international travellers (Americans virtually book it out, cruise after cruise) and Aussies are just opening up to the idea of seeing their own country from the water. All aboard, I say.

WHAT TO DO WHEN IN THE AREA

∞ On board, there's a gymnasium, hair and beauty salon, jacuzzi, cocktail bar, library, mud room, observation lounge, outdoor cafe, restaurant, sporting facilities, sun deck and health spa. You'll never have nothing to do.

∞ Other cruises are: Kimberley/East Timor/Arnhem Land, Papua New Guinea, World Heritage Reef, Antarctica. So you can go again and again.

MY TIP

Orion has just started taking people to Mount Borradaile, which is east of the Alligator River in Arnhem Land. Less than 1,000 people are granted access to this area each year and it's like a microcosm of Kakadu. The artwork there dates back 50,000 years and there are crocs like you'd never believe.

GETTING THERE

Climb aboard the gangplank wherever it's berthed.

ORION EXPEDITION CRUISES
26 Alfred Street, Milsons Point NSW 2061
P: 02 9033 8700 W: www.orioncruises.com.au

PORT CAMPBELL TO PORT FAIRY

When it comes to great drives, the Great Ocean Road is one of our best. I've travelled it for work and holidays and I still catch my breath whenever I see this rugged coastline. The road stretches for several hundred kilometres from Geelong to the South Australian border. It's surprisingly long, so here I'll take you from port to port (check out Autumn for the Torquay to Apollo Bay run).

Port Campbell is home to the Twelve Apostles with their glorious names: London Bridge, Bay of Islands and Loch Ard Gorge. This ripper coastline was sculpted over millions of years – they're literally the rock stars of the coast.

The Shipwreck Coast sounds dramatic, doesn't it? The waters truly do look wild as you make your way to Warrnambool. At Warrnambool a stunning sound and laser show at Flagstaff Hill will transport you back to the nineteenth century. For cheese lovers, I can't not mention Cheese World – your tummy will thank me for it. Nearby Tower Hill is home to an extinct volcano and bushwalks where you're guaranteed to see koalas, roos and maybe even emus. It's also a good place to learn about the region's Aboriginal history. You can even try some bushtucker while you're there.

At Port Fairy and Portland you will get a taste of life in a seafaring village. The well-kept old pubs and colonial buildings are a credit to these towns. At Port Fairy, take the track out to the lighthouse on Griffiths Island. As dusk falls you'll see thousands and thousands of mutton birds flying in to feed their young.

My last tip is for horse-lovers. Evoke the days of the light horsemen at Rundells Horse Riding stable and bolt along a perfect beach with the wind in your hair and as free as a bird. It's a wonderful way to experience this magnificent coast.

GETTING THERE

Loads of day-tripping tourist buses do the route, but there is so much to see, I'd advise you to spend more time and self-drive. Make your way to Geelong, and happy touring.

If you can, see the Twelve Apostles from a boat or plane. It gives a whole different perspective of the coastline: you can just see the ocean carving new sculptures in the limestone, and caves already formed in the rugged cliffs.

WHAT TO DO WHEN IN THE AREA

∞ Dive down deep; it's estimated that over 700 ships met a grisly end along the Shipwreck Coast.

∞ Explore all the state and national parks in the regions; there are heaps.

∞ Just as summer closes, Port Fairy hosts a four-day folk music festival, where you really need to book in advance for both tickets and accommodation – it has become that popular.

GREAT OCEAN ROAD
W: www.greatoceanroad.org

FLAGSTAFF HILL MARITIME VILLAGE
Merri Street, Warrnambool 3280
P: 03 5564 7841 W: www.flagstaffhill.com

CHEESE WORLD
Great Ocean Road, Allansford 3277
P: 03 5563 2130 W: www.cheeseworld.com.au

TOWER HILL STATE GAME RESERVE
Off Princes Highway, Koroit 3282
P: 13 1963 W: www.parkweb.vic.gov.au

RUNDELLS HORSE RIDING
78 Hodgetts Road, Portland 3305
P: 03 5529 2303 W: www.rundellshr.com.au

OR VISIT: www.visitvictoria.com

PORT MACQUARIE

Port Macquarie on the mouth of the Hastings River has 13 beaches, a glorious temperate climate and is one of Australia's best-loved coastal destinations. I have many happy memories of holidaying here as a child, enjoying the beaches, rainforests and hinterland. The best thing: it's value-packed. I took the challenge to spend a whole weekend at Port Macquarie with a family of four and only $500 to spend and we came home with change!

Cafe 66 is an award-winning Italian joint that didn't hurt the hip pocket and I loved the Pancake Place where kids rule. Timbertown, a recreation of a 1900s settler's town was adored by the children, especially the steam train ride and Cobb & Co coaches, particularly when a bit of whip-cracking was thrown in. Unbelievably, the entry was free. Hydro Golf and Mini Putt Putt was embarrassing for me (I'm so uncoordinated) but a hit with the others. Kids Crazy Maze was perfect for the nippers to wander around while we downed coffees. If you add in the coastal walks, the beaches (Flynns and Town get my thumbs up) and my favourite nature spot, Kooloonbung Creek Nature Park – a koala hospital run by volunteers where you really can't leave without adopting a sick or orphaned koala – what you get is a great holiday town with loads of wonderful, fun options.

MY TIP

Ever wanted to stay in a lighthouse? Smoky Cape is one of the best and it is not too far from Port Macquarie. It's got everything: knockout views, close to the beach and bush, perfect for families . . . but I'm sure it's haunted!

GETTING THERE

The 402 km drive from Sydney is a long-haul trip, but pit-stops at Newcastle, Nelson Bay and Forster make for cheap and cheerful detours. Port Macquarie is also well-serviced by train, buses and planes.

WHAT TO DO WHEN IN THE AREA

∞ All the beach things: swimming, surfing, sandcastle building, beach volleyball, and more.

∞ Great national parks and reserves in the area, so check them out with the visitor's centre.

∞ Plenty of places that offer horseriding and other rural activities; this area is beach and countryside all wrapped into one.

GREATER PORT MACQUARIE VISITOR CENTRE
P: 1300 303 155 W: www.portmacquarieinfo.com.au

CAFE 66
66 Clarence Street, Port Macquarie 2444
P: 02 6583 7117

PANCAKE PLACE
Cnr Clarence and Hay streets, Port Macquarie 2444
P: 02 6583 4544

TIMBERTOWN HERITAGE PARK
Oxley Highway, Wauchope 2446
P: 02 6586 1940 W: www. timbertown.com.au

HYDRO GOLF & PUTT PUTT
Boundary Street, Port Macquarie 2444
P: 02 6583 3200

KOALA HOSPITAL & STUDY CENTRE
Macquarie Nature Reserve, Lord St, Port Macquarie 2444
P: 02 6584 1522 W: www.koalahospital.org.au

SMOKY CAPE LIGHTHOUSE
Lighthouse Road, Arakoon, South West Rocks 2431
P: 02 6566 6301 W: www.smokycapelighthouse.com

OR VISIT: www.visitnsw.com.au

QUIRINDI & TAMWORTH REGION

I have to admit, I'm a bit biased towards Quirindi; it's my Dad's hometown. If you're craving country then Quirindi is pretty much the real deal. I had a moment of perfection here while giving a speech one Australia Day about what I loved about our lifestyle. As I looked out on the crowd, sitting on the green showground grass in front of me with the sun setting behind the Liverpool Ranges, I realised these people were living a life that's the envy of the world.

Quirindi has wonderful parks, a rich agricultural heritage and, as my Dad says, it's 'the birthplace of remarkable people'. The heritage village is open on weekends and has a great restaurant. Werris Creek, just 15 minutes north of the town, has the interesting Railway Monument with memorabilia dating back to the days when trains were the main source of transport through the region. My family and I love the First Fleet Gardens at Wallabadah. If a farm stay is on the agenda, definitely give Castle Mountain, a beautiful homestead smack dab in the bush, a try.

If you're around during January, scoot on up to Tamworth, in your boots of course, and join nearly 60,000 other festive folk at the Country Music Festival. It's great fun, with over 800 artists and nearly as many buskers singing their little hearts out. Dancing, bush poetry and every genre of country music . . . what are you waiting for?

WHAT TO DO WHEN IN THE AREA

∞ Take a look at the Quirindi town clock, a memorial to those who served in the First World War.

∞ Take a drive through the plains in the area and get a feel for what it must have been like when the early settlers arrived.

∞ Visit Willow Tree, a small arts and antiques village about 14 km south of Quirindi.

MY TIP

Quirindi is pretty flat but the Who'd-a-thought-it Lookout offers the best view of The Great Dividing Range as well as the richest agricultural land in NSW. It's just beautiful.

GETTING THERE

Quirindi is in the heart of Liverpool Ranges, 16 km off the New England Highway. That's about a four-hour drive northwest of Sydney by car, or 45 minutes south of Tamworth.

QUIRINDI TOURIST INFORMATION CENTRE
248 George Street, Quirindi 2343
P: 02 6746 2128

AUSTRALIAN RAILWAY MONUMENT
Single Street, Werris Creek 2341
P: 02 6768 7464

FIRST FLEET MEMORIAL GARDENS
New England Highway, Wallabah 2343
P: 02 6746 1755 W: www.lpsc.nsw.gov.au

CASTLE MOUNTAIN FARMSTAY
Quirindi 2343
P: 02 6746 2102 W: www.castlemountain.com.au

OR VISIT: www.visitnsw.com.au

SNOWY MOUNTAINS

Kosciuszko might be one of Australia's top ski destinations but it also dazzles during the summertime. Way back when, our family would book a lodge and we kids would drive Mum mad trying to conquer one outdoor activity after another. I have vivid memories of the wildflowers, the snow gums and the unrivalled beauty of the mountains. The alpine climate at this time of year is also wonderful; it lacks the humidity of other places and then cools down to 'just right' in the evening.

Horseriding is big here. You can take a trail ride for an hour or so, or embark on the full 'Man From Snowy River' experience for several days. Either way, you're guaranteed panoramic views and wildlife. Fishermen are spoilt for choice with 16 major dams to choose from to catch their trout, and then there are all sorts of rivers and streams. The gravel roads of the Snowys are loved by 4WD enthusiasts and mountain bike riders alike and the giant granite rocks set a challenge to any abseiler or climber. The caving is also brilliant.

At Lake Crackenback there are canoes for hire, and also ask about the nearby bobsledding. There are lots of guided walks that depart from Kosciuszko Alpine, some making full use of the old historic huts that dot the landscape. I do feel slightly guilty admitting this, but I'm also happy to just chill in the village of Thredbo, with its chalets and shops. It's an alpine resort with lots on offer . . . did I mention the shops?

Basically, stop thinking of alpine destinations just for the snow. These villages offer a great summer alternative – they are massive outdoor adventure parks.

WHAT TO DO WHEN IN THE AREA

∞ Lake Crackenback also offers golf, an indoor swimming pool, archery and tennis. Almost too much to choose from!

∞ Thredbo has a fantastic Blues Festival in January and great whitewater rafting.

MY TIP

Take a picnic to Dead Horse Gap to see wild brumbies in the distance – a very 'Man From Snowy River' moment.

GETTING THERE

Lake Crackenback is an easy two-hour drive from Canberra, and the nearest airport is at Cooma.

TOURISM SNOWY MOUNTAINS
W: www.snowymountains.com.au

LAKE CRACKENBACK RESORT
P: 02 6451 3000/1800 020 524
W: www.novotellakecrackenback.com.au

THREDBO ALPINE RESORT CENTRE
Friday Drive, Thredbo Village 2625
P: 02 6459 4100 W: www.thredbo.com.au

OR VISIT: www.visitnsw.com.au

STANLEY

'The Nut', 'The Christmas Cake', 'Tassie's Answer to Uluru' – I'm talking about the most dramatic natural feature of this cute little historic town, and everyone seems to have an opinion about it. It's just so obvious. As you enter town this massive, cliffy, round lump protrudes 150 metres up out of the water and you can't help but be drawn to it. I think it's an energy thing, and certainly the town revolves around this 13 million-year-old blob, formed when lava shot out from the surface and cooled to form the basalt monolith. For centuries it has sheltered Aborigines, guided many a wayward ship, and been home to millions of migratory birds. But it darn near killed me when I took the chairlift up and I was nearly blown straight off. It does make for a good story, though.

Stanley sits right out on a peninsula and looks out over Bass Strait. Every time I visit, the weather turns wild and I have a wicked time. It is the main fishing port on the northwest coast of Tasmania and, yes, the seafood here is mouthwatering. Creativity also flows thick and fast in this neck of the woods; there are galleries and gift shops aplenty. My fave is the Touchwood Craft Gallery where you can also grab a good coffee while you decide on your purchase. The pubs in this town are tops and no one seems to mind when you stumble in looking like a windswept wreck. Stanley has no traffic lights or parking meters and, although it might look sweet from the street, the energy of that Nut has everyone gunning for a good time . . . Stanley really does rock!

MY TIP

Sign up for a Tasmanian Devil Tour; it's quite spooky. You head out into the forest at night and see these wicked creatures in their own living room, up close and personal.

GETTING THERE

Stanley is in the northwest of Tasmania. You can boat in, or fly in, or take the scenic drive route.

WHAT TO DO WHEN IN THE AREA

∞ Catch the chairlift or walk up The Nut; it's hair-blowingly good fun.

∞ West Inlet is ideal for swimming, fishing and relaxing.

∞ Seaquarium exhibits range from shark tanks to rock pools. Great way to see a wide range of sealife.

∞ Seal and penguin tours operate form the wharf area during summer.

STANLEY VISITOR CENTRE
Main Road, Stanley 7331
P: 03 6458 1330

TOUCHWOOD CRAFT GALLERY & COFFEE SHOP
31 Church Street, Stanley 7331
P: 03 6458 1348 W: www.touchwoodstanley.com.au

HOLLOW BONES WILDLIFE EXPERIENCE
P: 0438 564 144

NUT CHAIRLIFT & INFORMATION CENTRE
Browns Road, Stanley 7331
P: 03 6458 1286

SEAQUARIUM
Fisherman's Dock, Stanley 7331
P: 03 6458 2052

BEACHSIDE RETREAT WEST INLET
West Inlet, 253 Stanley Highway, Stanley 7331
P: 03 6458 1350 W: www.beachsideretreat.com

OR VISIT: www.tourismtasmania.com.au

LORD NELSON
BREWERY HOTEL
SYDNEY'S OLDEST HOTEL
FIRST LICENSED 1841

SYDNEY

So, you only have time for a whistle-stop tour of Sydney? Then here's your checklist of surefire winners.

Okay, let's start with the one thing everyone must do – climb 'the Coathanger'. I've climbed it every which way, even illegally as a teen, and it's always a thrill. Dawn or dusk are the best times, and don't forget to wave to all the workaholics driving beneath you. You can now also climb around the Sydney Tower – 260 metres up with unforgettable 360-degree views.

Then head to The Strand for a one-stop shop. Stop at the Lindt Cafe for the best hot chocolate outside of Switzerland and make your way down to the Opera House for the backstage tour – you were born for that stage. Take a wander around The Rocks for a bit of Sydney's heritage and have a break at The Lord Nelson Hotel, where they brew the beers on site and serve a pretty tasty ploughman's lunch. Scoot back to Circular Quay to catch a ferry ride to Manly to continue your pub crawl at the hot Manly Wharf Hotel.

Our best weekend markets are at Glebe, Balmain, Paddington and Bondi. In Paddington my favourite shopping street is William, where you can pick up anything from Collette Dinnigan to recycled designer duds. At Bondi, the Icebergs on Notts Avenue is where I take English friends, show them the billion-dollar view and say, 'Can you believe you sent us here as convicts?'

MY TIP

In Sydney you have to get wet at the famous beaches and equally famous public pools: Boy Charlton by the Botanic Gardens and North Sydney under the bridge, to name two.

GETTING THERE

Sydney is midway along the east coast of Australia. There are a myriad of ways to get there and to get around once you're in the city, even via shank's pony.

WHAT TO DO WHEN IN THE AREA

∞ It's a major international city, full of theatres, sporting facilities and just damn fine restaurants and bars. Enjoy!

∞ The Observatory Hotel is my accommodation pick: it's central, luxurious, and even if you can't stay, try to sample the pool and spa.

SYDNEY BRIDGECLIMB
5 Cumberland Street, The Rocks 2000
P: 02 8274 7777 W: www.bridgeclimb.com

SYDNEY TOWER SKYWALK
Centrepoint Podium Level, 100 Market Street, Sydney 2000
P: 02 9333 9222 W: www.skywalk.com.au

THE STRAND ARCADE
Pitt Street Mall, Sydney 2000
W: www.standarcade.com.au

LINDT CAFE
Martin Place, Level 1, 53 Philip Street, Sydney 2000
P: 02 8257 1600

SYDNEY OPERA HOUSE
Bennelong Point, Sydney 2000
P: 02 9250 7111 W: www.sydneyoperahouse.com

LORD NELSON HOTEL
19 Kent Street, Sydney
P: 02 9251 4044

BONDI ICEBERGS
1 Notts Avenue, Bondi Beach 2026
P: 02 9365 9000 W: www.icebergs.com.au

OR VISIT: www.visitnsw.com.au

AUTUMN

ADELAIDE

I've always liked it here – the lively central markets, grazing on gastronomical treats at Gouger Street, and heading to nearby Glenelg to swim with the dolphins (yes, right near the city!). But the day I fell in love with this town was when I hopped on the Adelaide Explorer bus and saw the city in an orderly fashion. I wasn't quite sure where to go, or how to get there, but this gave me my bearings. Have a chat to the driver (well, I did) and you'll learn about the history of many sights – did you know the rose window at St Peter's Cathedral is identical to the one at Notre Dame in Paris?

Adelaide is rich in art and culture. A highlight for me was a backstage tour of the Festival Centre. The volunteer there was full of stories about some of the world's biggest performers; I even got to see dancers rehearsing. Exhibitions of local artists can be found at the JamFactory. I toured their workshops and ended up commissioning a young girl to make a gift to post home. Artlab, in a massive building on the edge of town, conserve cultural heritage from both here and abroad. During my trip they were restoring Captain Cook's suitcase and a statue from a city park. On clinic days you can take in your own treasures for an expert opinion.

Talking to locals, I found out that many are returning home to live. They'd gone east for a bit of career action, but are lured back by the promise of an amazing quality of life for half the cost of the eastern states. That's high praise.

MY TIP

The best thing I did was buy the Discover Adelaide Card that got me on the Explorer Bus, behind-the-scenes of the venues and discount passes to top attractions. Pretty cool.

GETTING THERE

Bang in the middle of the southern coastline of Australia, Adelaide is a bit of a drive west from Melbourne, or east from Perth. You can easily fly in, or hop on a train or bus.

WHAT TO DO WHEN IN THE AREA

∞ Rosa Matto Cookery School brings the markets alive. This local takes you to her favourite stalls, talking about and collecting ingredients along the way, then you go back to her studio to whip it all up – shop, learn, chat, eat; a great day out.

∞ Adelaide has a wonderful Botanic Gardens, and it's the site of WOMADelaide in early March.

∞ For another dose of culture, go when the biannual Arts Festival is on in early autumn.

∞ Autumn is also great for bookworms, when the Adelaide Writers' Festival kicks off.

∞ Rundle Mall is the heart of the city, and where you'll find loads of shops.

ADELAIDE CENTRAL MARKETS
Between Grote and Grouger streets, Adelaide 5000
P: 08 8203 7203
W: www.adelaide.sa.gov.au/centralmarket

ADELAIDE EXPLORER TOURS
60 Everard Avenue, Keswick 5035
P: 08 8293 2966 W: www.adelaideexplorer.com.au

ST PETER'S CATHEDRAL
27 King William Road, North Adelaide 5006
W: www.stpeters-cathedral.org

ADELAIDE FESTIVAL CENTRE
King William Road, Adelaide 5000
P: 08 8216 8600 W: www.afct.org.au

JAMFACTORY
19 Morphett Street, Adelaide 5000
P: 08 8410 0727 W: www.jamfactory.com.au

ARTLAB AUSTRALIA
70 Kintore Avenue, Adelaide 5000
P: 08 8207 7520 W: www.artlab.sa.gov.au

DISCOVER ADELAIDE CARD
P: 08 8400 2222 W: www.adelaidecard.com.au

ROSA MATTO COOKERY SCHOOL
2A Union Street, Goodwood 5034
P: 08 8373 6106 W: www.rosamatto.com

OR VISIT: **www.southaustralia.com**

BEECHWORTH

I was first lured here while on the trail of bushranger Ned Kelly. His Mum, Ellen, spent time in the town's imposing gaol and Ned made several appearances in the courthouse. I don't think much has changed since Ned's day as this town is proud to protect its history. But let me reassure you, there's plenty happening behind the National Trust-protected shopfronts.

Go into any pub and mix with the locals for all the town goss and definitely wander up to Wardens for a yarn and a scrumptious meal – Rocco and Lisa Esposito reel in the awards. I love to sit at their streetside tables, with the world's best coffee in hand, watching life (and the odd vintage car) go by. Another award-winner is the Beechworth Bakery. The pies, pastries and layout are impressive, and the owner is literally inspirational – buy his motivational book on the way out!

Something I found intriguing was the former asylum on top of the hill that's now the successful La Trobe hotel. People were locked up here for things like refusing to answer a police sergeant's or judge's question! The stories are riveting and the place is haunted, for sure. The magnificent heritage gardens surrounding the site are believed to have been designed by a former patient – a sheer genius, I think.

One more place that makes me weak at the knees is the Black Springs Bakery B&B. The town of Black Springs once stood here but the bakery is all that remains. Today it's home to four hectares of French-inspired gardens and one of those cottages you just wish you could take home with you.

MY TIP

In May, Beechworth comes alive with the Harvest Festival, reliving the highs and lows of the gold rush days, and local producers showcase their delicious regional treats.

GETTING THERE

Located 270 km northeast of Melbourne, access is via the Hume Freeway.

WHAT TO DO WHEN IN THE AREA

∞ Visit Beechworth Provender for regional gourmet produce.

∞ Murray Breweries produce old-fashioned cordials.

∞ The streets are lined with over 30 National Trust listed heritage buildings to explore; join the Legends Walking Tour to check them all out.

BEECHWORTH VISITOR CENTRE
Town Hall, Ford Street, Beechworth 3747
P: 03 5728 8065/1300 366 321
W: www.beechworthonline.com.au

BEECHWORTH HISTORIC COURT HOUSE
94 Ford Street, Beechworth 3747
P: 03 5728 2721

WARDENS FOOD AND WINE
32 Ford Street, Beechworth 3747
P: 03 5728 1377

BEECHWORTH BAKERY
27 Camp Street, Beechworth 3747
P: 03 5728 1132 W: www.beechworthbakery.com

LA TROBE AT BEECHWORTH
Albert Road, Beechworth 3747
P: 03 5720 8050 W: www.latrobeatbeechworth.com.au

BEECHWORTH LEGENDS WALKING TOUR
P: 03 5728 2031/1300 366 321
W: www.tourisminternet.com.au/bwwalk1.htm

BLACK SPRINGS BAKERY PROVINCIAL ESCAPE
464 Wangaratta Road, Beechworth 3747
P: 03 5728 2565 W: www.blackspringsbakery.com

OR VISIT: **www.visitvictoria.com**

BERRY

As far as cute country towns go, Berry is right up there. Loved by Sydneysiders for weekend jaunts, it is the very definition of a short, pleasurable getaway. Shoppers go nuts over Berry. I'm sure they're lulled into a false sense of calm due to the fresh country air, but make sure your credit card is not maxed out before you embark on a stroll down Queen Street; it's absolutely chockers with shops overflowing with nothing you need but everything you just can't live without.

To start, pop into Broughton Antiques for that 'I'll find room for it somewhere' piece. Then drop by the Berry Bakery, which has more pastries than your tummy can handle. The publican of the Great Southern Hotel will keep you amused with stories while he pours you a restorative, and you have to sample the regional fruits at Silos – yum! After all that, you'll no doubt end up exhausted and collapsed on a park bench.

One more tip is to head into the surrounding region. Work off those pastries with nature walks and don't be surprised if you share the path with a family of wombats. The hinterland is also home to wonderful chalets and cottages that look out across lush valleys, often with the sea on the horizon. Seven Mile Beach has legendary status in the area but only a short drive along a country lane or two will take you to Werri, Gerroa and Gerringong beaches.

Okay, so I can't tell you about any wicked nightclubs in or near Berry, but who needs them when you can have a spree like this in the best of country locales?

MY TIP

Keep an eye out for the famous Berry Donut Van at the end of Queen Street. This is no dunkin' type of doughnut, it's the true, original variety – Mmmmmm.

GETTING THERE

Only 16 km from Nowra, it's an easy drive from Sydney and Canberra, and buses between them regularly stop here.

WHAT TO DO WHEN IN THE AREA

∞ Berry's Monthly Markets at the Berry Showground are the place to be on the first Sunday of each month. Then there's the Flea Markets at the Great Southern Hotel on the third Sunday of the month – shopaholic heaven!

∞ In May, the annual Berry Quilt & Craft Show at the Berry School of Arts gives you a chance to admire this timeless tradition.

∞ You're surrounded here by lush rolling countryside, so head out for a drive. You can stop at Open Gardens, cafes and even the odd second-hand bookshop along the way. Explore!

BROUGHTON ANTIQUES
118 Queen Street, Berry 2535
P: 02 4464 1036

BERRY BAKERY
110 Queen Street, Berry 2535
P: 02 4464 1122

GREAT SOUTHERN HOTEL
95 Queen Street, Berry 2535
P: 02 4464 1009

SILOS RESTAURANT
B640 Princes Highway, Jaspers Brush, near Berry 2535
P: 02 4448 6160   W: www.silos.com.au

BERRY CHAMBER OF COMMERCE AND INDUSTRY
P: 02 4464 3122   W: www.berry.org.au

OR VISIT: www.visitnsw.com.au

CANBERRA

If, like me, you're someone who revels in seeing seasons change then visit Canberra in autumn. It's very pretty. The parks and gardens are lush and colourful and it's also chilly enough to get cosy in front of a roaring fire. A particularly good one to stoke is at the historic Hotel Kurrajong (where a certain Ben Chifley lived when he was prime minister).

A new experience for me was sampling the district's wine-making region. Helm at Murrumbateman (try saying that after a couple of chardies) is impressive – Ken and Judith are fourth generation descendants of German winegrowers. Their tasting room is actually in an old schoolhouse which dates back to 1888! Once you've bought your vino, head to Kingston or Manuka, Canberra's answer to Toorak or Double Bay, for all the cool restaurants and cafes. Filthy Gorgeous in Kingston (love saying that) has live music on weekends.

On a serious note, the War Museum is incredibly moving. Designed by C.E.W. Bean as a place where families and friends can grieve for loved ones buried in places far away, everyone leaves here with a clearer understanding of the tragedies of war. Don't forget to also take a peek inside the National Library. The last exhibition I visited had everything from Captain Cook's *Endeavour* journal to prototype sketches of the good ol' Aussie Holden. Oh, and you can even research your family tree while you're there.

MY TIP

Hot air balloon it right over Parliament House; it's a very smooth and gentle way to see the city from high. With its gentle glide, it's perfect for taking photographs. The Balloon Fiesta over Easter is a great time to fly.

GETTING THERE

As the nation's capital, Canberra is well-serviced by air, road and rail. It's only a three-hour drive from Sydney; seven hours from Melbourne.

WHAT TO DO WHEN IN THE AREA

∞ The National Gallery is my mild obsession; you've got to check out the permanent exhibition with Pollack's Blue Poles, and keep an eye out for the children's exhibits.

∞ Not one, but two parliament houses have something to offer. Why not take a seat in the public gallery at the 'new' one to see the so-called adults at play. And check out the portraits at the 'old' one.

∞ In early April there's a District Wine Harvest Festival; great for sampling the local tipples.

HOTEL KURRAJONG
National Circuit, Barton 2600
P: 02 6234 4444 W: www.hotelkurrajong.com.au

HELM WINES
Butts Road, Murrumbateman 2582
P: 02 6227 5953 W: www.helmwines.com.au

FILTHY GORGEOUS
8 Macpherson Street, O'Connor 2602
P: 02 6162 0033

AUSTRALIAN WAR MEMORIAL
Treloar Crescent, Campbell 2612
P: 02 6243 4211 W: www.awm.gov.au

NATIONAL LIBRARY OF AUSTRALIA
Parkes Place, Parkes 2600
P: 02 6262 1111 W: www.nla.gov.au

DAWN DRIFTERS—CANBERRA BALLOON FLIGHTS
Shop 10, Curtin Plaza, Curtin 2605
P: 02 6285 4450 W: www.dawndrifters.com.au

NATIONAL GALLERY OF AUSTRALIA
Parkes Place, Parkes 2600
P: 02 6240 6502 W: www.nga.gov.au

PARLIAMENT HOUSE
Capital Hill, Canberra 2600
P: 02 6277 5399 W: www.aph.gov.au

NATIONAL PORTRAIT GALLERY
Old Parliament House, King George Terrace, Parkes 2600
P: 02 6270 8236 W: www.portrait.gov.au

OR VISIT: www.canberratourism.com.au

CENTRAL COAST

My, how you've changed! That's what I think when I return to my childhood holiday beaches: Terrigal, Avoca and Ettalong. People have now realised they can easily commute to manic Sydney in an hour and still have their laidback Central Coast lifestyle, with its big surf and golden beaches. This 'best of both worlds' attitude has seen the area boom.

Terrigal is kinda like the hip part of the Central Coast. It has a youthful vibe and great nightlife and restaurants. The Crowne Plaza Hotel is great, but if you have children Star of the Sea is brilliant. No matter what your age, clamber to the top of The Skillion, try not to be blown off, then race down to the bottom, arms outstretched, free as a seagull.

Avoca is slightly quieter but has the beautiful Lighthouse Apartments with the best views and just a quick stroll to the beach! One memory I love to relive is the Avoca flicks. The cinema never changes. As a child I literally rolled Jaffas down the aisle; as a teen the outdoor movie nights rocked; now I revel in its classic charm . . . I hope it never alters.

The sleepy seaside village of Ettalong has quite happily stayed under the radar while Terrigal and Avoca have stolen the limelight. But the Outrigger Resort, front and centre on the main beach, makes it near impossible for it to hide its light under a bushel any more. Tourists are loving it.

The laidback pace of the Aussie coastal life is such a wonderful equaliser. Just relax and enjoy it.

MY TIP

The Avoca Beach Hotel is great for us meat lovers and you can't go past T-Bone Tuesday. They serve a steak so big it nearly moos – just thought you'd like to know.

GETTING THERE

Well serviced by buses and trains, you take the freeway north of Sydney and you're there in an hour, or an hour and a half. Or a ferry leaves Palm Beach every 90 minutes for Ettalong.

WHAT TO DO WHEN IN THE AREA

∞ Puccinos in Ettalong is known for the best brunch and atmosphere in the region.

∞ Go trekking through the Brisbane Waters and Bouddi National Park.

∞ Immerse yourself in the Ettalong markets every weekend.

CROWNE PLAZA HOTEL
Pine Tree Lane, Terrigal 2260
P: **02 4384 9111**   W: **www.crowneplazaterrigal.com.au**

STAR OF THE SEA LUXURY APARTMENTS
8 The Esplanade, Terrigal 2260
P: **02 4385 7979**   W: **www.staroftheseaterrigal.com**

LIGHTHOUSE APARTMENTS AT AVOCA BEACH
3/15 Cliff Avenue, Avoca Beach 2250
P: **02 4382 1311**   W: **www.georgebrand.com.au**

AVOCA THEATRE
69 Avoca Drive, Avoca Beach 2251
P: **02 4381 1488**   W: **www.avocatheatre.com.au**

ETTALONG BEACH TOURIST RESORT (OUTRIGGER)
Cnr Ocean View and Schnapper roads, Ettalong Beach 2257
P: **02 4341 1999**   W: **www.ettalongbeachtouristresort.com.au**

PUCCINOS
Shop 40, 189 Ocean View Drive, Ettalong Beach 2257
P: **02 4342 8052**

OR VISIT: **www.visitnsw.com.au**

CRADLE MOUNTAIN

Okay, we all have to agree the Cradle Mountain/Lake St Clair National Park is mind-blowing, which is why it's on the World Heritage list. If you've only got time to explore one section of Tassie wilderness, I vote you choose this one. The local guides are exceptional; proud to show off their backyard with a genuine love of the place. The landscape will have your heart soaring and the mountain air is better than any facial money can buy.

The one real quandary you face before you get here is how best to experience the 125,000 hectares of icy lakes and rugged mountains. Do you want to tough it out with the best of them? Hike, then camp and sleep in a communal hut that could perhaps reek of the previous night's baked beans? Or stay in an environmentally friendly wooden cabin, heated, of course, with hot showers, a cosy bed and a glass of local vino waiting for you after your 12-kilometre walk? I know what I'd prefer to do: Cradle Mountain Huts all the way!

This is a bushwalker's heaven – you can follow the same trail for 80 km without crossing a road and spend a night in comfort on the way. There are vistas of rugged mountain peaks, perfectly still and clear lakes, the impressive King Billy Pines with ancient forests and awesome beauty. There's nearly a trek for every fitness level, expert guides and a nice place to sleep at the end of the day – sound appealing? As one lady said to me, 'It's kind of like walking from one hotel suite to another'. I'm with her – it's just pure luxury out in the middle of the wilderness.

WHAT TO DO WHEN IN THE AREA

∞ You can hire a mountain bike and go for a ride if you're feeling really energetic.

∞ I've always loved a good spa, and the Waldheim Alpine Spa is a real treat after a day's excursion.

∞ Native animal night-viewing tours are easily arranged, and fun to boot.

∞ Try canoeing on Dove Lake – this must be how it felt at the beginning of time.

∞ The Park runs a shuttle bus between Cradle Mountain Visitor Centre and Dove Lake.

MY TIP

Do yourself a favour and don't buy new hiking boots for this trip – the blisters just aren't worth it.

GETTING THERE

About a two-hour drive from Launceston, the nearest airport; four hours northwest of Hobart.

VOYAGES CRADLE MOUNTAIN LODGE
Cradle Mountain/Lake St Clair National Park
P: 03 6492 1303 W: www.cradlemountainlodge.com.au

CRADLE MOUNTAIN HUTS
Cradle Mountain/Lake St Clair National Park
P: 03 6391 9339 W: www.cradlehuts.com.au

PARKS AND WILDLIFE SERVICE
4057 Cradle Mountain Road, Cradle Mountain 7310
P: 03 6492 1133/1300 135 513 W: www.parks.tas.gov.au

OR VISIT: www.discovertasmania.com.au

FRASER ISLAND

What could I possibly add to all the info already dispensed about Fraser Island? I'm sure you know it is World Heritage listed, includes miles upon miles of ancient rainforest – the only place in the world where it actually grows on sand – dozens of inland lakes and wicked wildlife. But did you know it's been voted as one of the world's 'sexiest islands'? Of course, that should come as no surprise as it has many nooks and crannies that are great for privacy, a perfect climate and sublime waters. I mean, there aren't too many places more sexy than Seventy-Five Mile Beach. It just goes on and on and on . . . The cliffs that frame it are the most beautiful colour and the sand dunes would definitely provide a lot of space and privacy in which to frolic.

I tend to head to the inland lakes and waterways for a dip. Try the swimming holes at the Champagne Pools, the refreshing Lake Wabby and the absolutely crystal-clear Lake McKenzie. You will also fall in love, and possibly lust, over the Kingfisher Bay Resort. My Nan was happy to just sit on her balcony there each day and watch the birdlife (354 species have been recorded on the island, not by Nan though) and she even spotted a turtle down by the shore.

Fraser is beautifully isolated so you'll be lucky to get a signal on your mobile, which means you can focus on your surroundings and your loved one. Now that is sexy.

MY TIP

Riding horseback along one of the world's most beautiful beaches has got to be sexy in anyone's book. We organised a special Clip Clop tour of Fraser and camped out.

GETTING THERE

By air or ferry from Hervey Bay or Rainbow Beach, just north of Noosa. There's also a ferry from Urangan Boat Harbour. The best way to get around Fraser is by 4WD, but you'll need a vehicle permit to take your own on to the island.

WHAT TO DO WHEN IN THE AREA

∞ Bushwalking, fishing, swimming and 4WD tours are the things to do.

∞ If you float down Eli Creek, it will carry you all the way to the beach. Just walk up alongside this crystal-clear freshwater creek and hop in.

∞ This place is wild: dingos roam free, but don't feed them; and also look out for migrating whales – only dangerous if you swim too close!

∞ Shipwrecks are aplenty in this neck of the woods. The most famous is the beached *Maheno*, which ran aground in 1935.

∞ Aboriginal sites such as the Pinnacles provide places for quiet reflection.

FRASER ISLAND WEBSITE
W: www.fraserisland.net

KINGFISHER BAY RESORT AND VILLAGE
P: 1800 072 555/07 4120 3333 W: www.kingfisherbay.com

OR VISIT: www.queenslandholidays.com.au

HAMILTON ISLAND

Visit Whitehaven Beach on the eastern side of an uninhabited island. The pristine environment is spectacular and the white silica sand is like walking on talcum powder.

I never wanted to fall for the charms of Hamilton – how could I possibly recommend an exquisite island that plopped a high-rise hotel right into the middle of it? It is way over the palm treeline and a bit of an eyesore. But when I was sent here to do a story I found I just couldn't resist the place. I fell hard. Let me explain why.

Firstly, it's so convenient. It's the only island with an airport, which makes it easy to arrive and to access the other 74 Whitsunday Islands quickly. But once here, passengers seem to want to stay on Hamilton because there are several great hotels to choose from and heaps of activities. The Beach Club Resort is to die for – it's luxurious and right on Catseye Beach, overlooking the Coral Sea. While they don't allow children, the Reef View can't get enough of them and they keep all their guests happy. That's perhaps why the island is continually voted one of the most family friendly. There's always a deal going where ankle-biters can 'stay, play and eat free'. How could parents not love that?

I also had no idea the island had so many restaurants. Down at Marina Village there's great Italian at Romano's through to cheeky Aussie pies at Bob's Bakery. Add a general store, several boutiques and a bank and you really don't need to leave the island. Getting around is fun as well. They have these really cute golf carts that, try as you might, are impossible to speed in.

But let's get back to why we all come here: the water, the beaches, the Whitsundays. You look around at all this beauty and it just doesn't matter where you stay, what you put in your tummy or how you get here. Just get here. What's not to love?

WHAT TO DO WHEN IN THE AREA

∞ There are daily tours to The Great Barrier Reef in glass-bottom boats and dive and snorkel cruise boats. A superb way to experience this incredible environment.

∞ Try sea kayaking, twilight sails, game fishing, scenic flights, waterskiing . . . the list is endless.

∞ Great bushwalking, and you can also cuddle a koala.

∞ The Relaxation Centre will give you a massage to get into that holiday mood; there's even early morning yoga sessions on the beach.

∞ For kids, the Clownfish Club is essential visiting.

GETTING THERE

Hamilton is the only island in the region with a commercial airport. There are more than 40 flights to this paradise every week, including direct flights from Melbourne, Sydney, Brisbane and Cairns. You can also hop on a shuttle boat at Shute Harbour or an air taxi from mainland towns nearby.

HAMILTON ISLAND
Whitsunday Islands, The Great Barrier Reef
P: 13 7333/02 9433 0444 W: www.hamiltonisland.com.au

FANTASEA CRUISES
11 Shute Harbour Road, Airlie Beach 4802
P: 07 4946 5111 W: www.fantasea.com.au

OR VISIT: www.queenslandholidays.com.au

HEPBURN SPRINGS

Hepburn Springs is the spa capital of Australia and home to the highest concentration of natural mineral water springs in the country. Since the early 1800s Victorians have made pilgrimages here to 'take to the waters'; these days there are a mass of retreats offering to pamper and indulge you in every which way. I find Hepburn a little bit quieter than its big sister Daylesford and the focus here is more on health and wellbeing, a definitive restorative.

The original bathhouse is Hepburn Spa and they offer all sorts of hydrotherapy treatments and tactile therapies. I like the simple massages where you look out onto the surrounding bushland. While other spas pipe 'bush music' into the room, here you have the real thing as you are literally among it. If you're keen you can take a self-guided walk through the bush to drink the waters straight from the springs. Authenticity is the key here.

There are fantastic pubs and cafes in Hepburn with live music on weekends. but if you'd like to take home a local pressie, bliss out at Lavandula Farm. I'm in awe of what owner Carol White has created here – field after field of this sweet-smelling plant, which children are free to romp through. The air is filled with the scent, instantly calming you, so appropriate for this peaceful neck of the woods. It's kind of like a pocket of French Provence in country Victoria. I found myself taking not only gardening notes but also cooking tips from the restaurant's chef. I've never tried lavender sausages, ice-cream or lemonade before, but now I'm hooked.

Hepburn is also picnic paradise – choose a paddock with a nice dry-stone wall, sit back and simply enjoy. No matter what time of year you visit, it's always beautiful here.

GETTING THERE

Just one and a half hours drive northwest of Melbourne, not far from Ballarat, Bendigo and Daylesford. Take the Western Freeway and Midland Highway.

WHAT TO DO WHEN IN THE AREA

∞ Mount Franklin is a volcanic crater with picnic spots, horseriding ranches and a blowhole. Ah, yes, it's also home to Mount Franklin mineral water.

∞ You can bottle your own mineral water for free from the hand pumps and pipes at the Mineral Springs Reserve.

∞ Play a round of golf at the local course, and remember to yell 'Fore' to the resident kangaroos – can't guarantee that they will understand you, though.

∞ Go for a bush walk – Tipperary Springs and Twin Bridges are my pick.

∞ In May the town holds the wonderful Swiss/Italian Festa, which is great fun.

MY
TIP

Nearby Cricket Willow is not only the home to the first Aussie-made cricket bats; they also hire out their cricket oval. It's the best day out! Get a side together; it's quite old school, with a picket fence, the mountains in the distance, plus a cricket museum and cafe.

**HEPBURN SPA MINERAL SPRINGS BATHHOUSE
& WELLNESS RETREAT**
1 Mineral Springs Reserve, Hepburn Springs 3461
P: 03 5348 8888 W: www.hepburnspa.com.au

OLD HEPBURN HOTEL
236 Main Road, Hepburn Springs 3461
P: 03 5348 2207 W: www.oldhepburnhotel.com.au

LAVANDULA SWISS ITALIAN FARM
350 Hepburn–Newstead Road, Shepherds Flat 3461
P: 03 5476 4393 W: www.lavandula.com.au

CRICKET WILLOW
355 Hepburn–Newstead Road, Shepherds Flat 3461
P: 03 5476 4277 W: www.cricketwillow.com.au

OR VISIT: www.visitvictoria.com

HUNTER VALLEY

The Hunter is so slick, stylish and abundant in every way that it can be a little bit overwhelming to know where to go. Remember, this is the oldest wine region in Australia; the Hunter basically invented wine tourism.

The Pepper Tree Estate is a one-stop shop and home to possibly the region's top restaurant and guesthouse, and a great tasting room. Robert and Sally Molines at Roberts have been dishing up scrumptious food in their rambling cottage here for over 20 years. The dishes are tasty, the flowers fresh and the staff happy: three ingredients for culinary success. A short stroll up the driveway takes you to the famous Convent Guest House, built in 1909 in Coonamble for an order of nuns and transported here in 1990. People stop to take photos of its exterior, but I recommend you stay. Sharon Evans, the cellar-door supervisor at Pepper Tree Wines, is a fount of knowledge, so stop and have a chat for the best wine tips.

For an amazing collection of French antiques visit Evans Family Wine and Antiques. If you like a bit of cheese with your wine, head to the Hunter Valley Cheese Company. The Hunter Valley Gardens are lovely, the Rose Garden is great for picnics, and I hear they have a moonlight cinema.

It amazes me that in the Hunter you can chat to the person whose name is on the bottle. At Tyrell's you'll no doubt find Bruce chatting to visitors about his family and grapes that date back to 1858. There's no pretension in the Hunter and ultimately that's its appeal.

MY TIP

Almost every winery has a picnic area and every food outlet will help you put a tasty picnic basket together to go with your wine choice.

GETTING THERE

Zip along the F3 Freeway from Sydney, follow the signs, and the Hunter's yours to enjoy.

WHAT TO DO WHEN IN THE AREA

∞ There are lots of ways to check out the wineries: bus tour, bicycle or limo. Leave the car behind and indulge in all the region has to offer.

∞ There are balloon rides and carriage tours to get a different perspective of the vineyards.

∞ Craft and gift centres offer great trinkets to take home to the rellos with those bottles of wine.

PEPPER TREE COMPLEX
86 Halls Road, Pokolbin 2320

ROBERTS RESTAURANT (AT PEPPER TREE)
P: 02 4998 7330 W: www.robertsrestaurant.com

PEPPERS CONVENT (GUEST HOUSE)
P: 02 4998 7764 W: www.peppers.com.au

PEPPER TREE WINES
P: 02 4998 7539 W: www.peppertreewines.com.au

EVANS FAMILY WINES AND ANTIQUES
Lot 91, Broke Road, Pokolbin 2320
P: 02 4998 7237

HUNTER VALLEY CHEESE COMPANY
Cnr Broke Road and McDonalds Road, Pokolbin 2320
P: 02 4998 7744 W: www.huntervalleycheese.com.au

HUNTER VALLEY GARDENS
Broke Road, Pokolbin 2320
P: 02 4998 4000 W: www.hvg.com.au

TYRRELL'S WINES
Broke Road, Pokolbin 2320
P: 02 4993 7000 W: www.tyrrells.com.au

OR VISIT: www.visitnsw.com.au

HYAMS BEACH

When your grand moment arrives and you're asked to be on the cover of Vogue, have the photo taken on Hyams Beach. The sand is so white you'll glow in its reflection! It's extraordinary, like talcum powder, soft to touch and so fine it squeaks when you walk on it. I know people obsessed with this area, waxing lyrical about it's quiet beauty, and so do I. This is the exclusive part of Jervis Bay.

There is only one general store in the area, called Jervis Blue, and it supplies wonderful gourmet food and, most importantly, great coffee. I just loved my cruise of the remote beaches on a kayak with the Jervis Bay Kayak Company. The crystal-clear waters are sheltered and extremely peaceful; virtually silent aside from nature. You quietly glide past one untouched landscape after another. The guides are knowledgeable, love their job and are great to talk to. Best of all, their state-of-the-art kayaks don't numb your derrière. Each one has a foot-operated rudder and a small storage compartment for personal items – they have simply thought of everything.

I really loved exploring the Booderee National Park this way. I thought I'd get bored with a whole day out on the water, but the smile never left my face. We stopped off at Murray's Beach for morning tea and a dip in the cool fresh water, and I remember being almost ticked off that there weren't more people out enjoying the day with us. When a place is this beautiful, it's only natural to want to share it.

MY TIP

For accommodation, Hyams Beach Seaside Cottages are almost on top of the beach, and the word is that number 96 is the most sought-after cottage for couples.

GETTING THERE

Only two and a half hours drive from Sydney. Head south on the Princes Highway and turn to the coast near Nowra.

WHAT TO DO WHEN IN THE AREA

∞ Dive Jervis Bay; it's a sheltered inlet close to the Continental Shelf.

∞ Explore the rocky cliffs of the area, looking out for dolphins in the ocean from these vantage points.

∞ Heaps of places to eat and relax in Jervis Bay, a veritable feast, and not too far away.

JERVIS BLUE CAFE RESTAURANT
76 Cyrus St, Hyams Beach 2540
P: 02 4443 3874

JERVIS BAY KAYAK COMPANY
Shop 7b, Campbell Court, Vincentia 2540
P: 02 4441 7157 W: www.jervisbaykayaks.com

BOODEREE NATIONAL PARK AND BOTANIC GARDENS
Village Road, Jervis Bay 2540
P: 02 4442 1006 W: www.deh.gov.au/parks/booderee

HYAMS BEACH SEASIDE COTTAGES
53–55 Cyrus St, Hyams Beach 2540
P: 02 4441 7838 W: www.hyamsbeachseasidecottages.com.au

OR VISIT: www.visitnsw.com.au

LAKE EYRE

The heart of Australia has inspired many great explorers with the promise of a rich, vast, inland sea. There's actually a whaling boat at Tibaburra, which an early pioneer was hoping to put to use when he sailed the elusive waters. Sadly, what they did not know is that Lake Eyre rarely fills. It's really a vast, dry salt pan, but what a salt pan!

This strange landscape is ever-changing, so no matter what time of year you visit it's a sight to see. In 1997 I saw it evolve into one of the world's largest inland lakes when water trickled up through its salty crust and lapped the desert. A remarkable sight – even David Attenborough's film crew arrived, fascinated by the rapidly changing ecological sytem. Fish, birds and all sorts of bizarre wildlife seemingly crawled out of the earth, lured by the promise of water.

The best way to appreciate it is from the air. We were able to also fly on to Witjira National Park where we landed at Dalhousie Springs. Once there, we swam at sunset in large pools of Artesian Basin water, which was naturally heated to 37 degrees. I still have the photos from that day on my fridge at home and you can see the steam rising from the water's surface.

A highlight for me was staying at the famous heritage-listed William Creek Hotel, which has to be the most remote pub in the country. We had a ball when all the station's jackaroos turned up for the shoot. Incidentally, they work on one of the world's biggest cattle stations in one of SA's smallest towns. William Creek hit the international stage in 1987 when the most expensive public phone in the world – the first to be solar-powered – was built there. That phone booth cost a cool $1.6 million; now that's an expensive call.

GETTING THERE

Travelling from Adelaide, Lake Eyre National Park is off the Oodnadatta Track, about 7 km southeast of William Creek. Witjira is reached via Port Augusta, Coober Pedy, Marla, Oodnadatta, Hamilton Station and on to Eringa or Dalhousie Springs. Wrights Air flies in to the area.

MY TIP

At William Creek Hotel, leave a personal item behind at the bar. They say they're happy with a business card, but won't say no to a bra or knickers.

WHAT TO DO WHEN IN THE AREA

∞ Camp to get a real feel for the isolation of the outback; the stars overhead are brighter than bright.

∞ Be in awe of your surroundings. This is true desert landscape and everything is so intense.

∞ Visit Bloods Creek windmill, Mt Dare Homestead and Purni Bore while at Witjira.

LAKE EYRE NATIONAL PARK AND
WITJIRA NATIONAL PARK (DALHOUSIE SPRINGS)
P: 1800 816 078 W: www.parks.sa.gov.au/lakeeyre

WILLIAM CREEK HOTEL
Oodnadatta Track, William Creek 5710
P: 08 8670 7880 W: www.williamcreekhotel.net.au

WRIGHTS AIR
P: 08 8670 7962 W: www.wrightsair.com.au

OR VISIT: www.southaustralia.com

MELBOURNE

I know, this is the most cosmopolitan city in Australia, with great theatre, fine dining, world-class sport and shopping, but how about those flowers! Melburnians love their gardens. Drive around suburbs like Toorak, Kew, Malvern and even Albert Park; the term 'low maintenance' does not come to mind, but 'romantic', 'rambling', 'eclectic' and 'stylish' do. You might see glorious camellias in a pretty courtyard garden, something wickedly modern or perhaps even a grand masterpiece from the famous garden designer Paul Bangay.

Autumn is such a fine time for us green thumbs to visit as this is when the biggest flower and garden show in the Southern Hemisphere – Melbourne International Flower and Garden Show – takes place. Melbourne is renowned for its four seasons, so the plants respond on cue; the Royal Exhibition Building and Carlton Gardens bloom into a technicolour display. It's considered one of the top five garden shows in the world.

My love for Melbourne's gardens, though, grew when I 'did the Tan', a walking track that encircles the glorious Botanic Gardens. No matter what the time of day, it's full of people checking out 36 hectares, 50,000 plants, lakes, wildlife . . . it's overwhelming. Reward yourself at the end with a coffee at the Observatory Cafe.

Recently, I took my godson Felix to the new Children's Garden there and watched him run riot among wetlands, bamboo forests, crazy water features and the kitchen garden created for city-based children who don't have the chance to connect with nature on a daily basis. The designers wanted to create an environment for little bodies with big imaginations. Judging by Felix's joy, they hit the jackpot. You never know – maybe it will inspire a whole new generation of greenthumbs. I hope so.

GETTING THERE

Both the show and the Botanic Gardens are in the Melbourne city region. Train, tram, car or bus will all get you there. It's only a quick stroll from the Arts Centre and Flinders Street.

WHAT TO DO WHEN IN THE AREA

∞ The Botanic Gardens hold special events all the time. Check their website or go the Visitors Centre in the Observatory Precinct.

∞ Go stargazing at the Old Melbourne Observatory in the grounds of the Gardens.

∞ Enjoy a bite at the cafes in the Gardens or bring your own picnic. Be careful of those waterbirds, who just might be hungry too.

MY TIP

Garden lovers who just can't get enough will adore day trips to Mount Macedon and the Dandenongs, and look out for Paul Bangay's annual open day at Wood End.

MELBOURNE INTERNATIONAL
FLOWER AND GARDEN SHOW
**Royal Exhibition Building and Carlton Gardens,
Nicholson Street, Carlton 3000**
P: **03 9864 1111** W: **www.melbflowershow.com.au**

ROYAL BOTANIC GARDENS MELBOURNE
Birdwood Avenue, South Yarra 3141
P: **03 9252 2300** W: **www.rbg.vic.gov.au**

OR VISIT: **www.visitvictoria.com**

MID NORTH COAST

Terry Schwamberg, the genius behind Contemporary Hotels and the lady with a knack for picking travel hot spots, looks for several things when seeking the next big destination. It has to be a beautiful locale, of course, have a strong youth culture, easy access by car or transport, the potential for great food and bevvies and interesting local architecture; plus a few tourist highlights. 'So, where is Madame Schwamberg's next Aussie tip?' Answer: the mid-north coast of NSW or, to be more specific, Pacific Palms.

Pacific Palms is on a strip of coast nestled between Myall Lakes and Forster. Nearby are the sublime beaches of Blueys, Boomerang, Elizabeth and Shelleys. Could you ask for anything more? Well, throw in Charlotte Bay, Green Point, Smiths Lake, Tarbuck Bay, Coomba Park, Seal Rocks (so in love with this spot), Cellito Beach, Booti Booti National Park, Wallingat State Forest and Wallis Lake, home to the famous oysters. This whole area is beautiful to drive around. And just pick a beach, any beach, and keep your eyes peeled for whales and dolphins. Or just watch the sail boats bob by and fishermen delight in their catch of the day.

Terry says she tends to be lured to a location by the thought, 'I'd love a beach house here'. Blueys has caught her eye with its pure sand and clear waters. I definitely recommend staying somewhere with an awesome ocean view.

The real appeal of the mid-north coast is that it still feels like a sleepy beachside retreat. Just how long it remains like that . . . well, we'll see.

MY TIP

Head to the Oyster Co-op near Wallace Lake to buy the tastiest, cheapest freshly shucked oysters.

GETTING THERE

The Pacific Palms region is about a three-hour drive north of Sydney.

WHAT TO DO WHEN IN THE AREA

∞ Hire a fully-equipped beach house and take lots of long, deep breaths. Smell that clean air.

∞ Beach hop, and with so many beaches on offer, surfing is big . . . even in nippy autumn!

∞ At Smiths Lake you can hire all manner of craft to cruise the sheltered waterway and rivers.

∞ Many villages to explore with lots of cafes to get that hot chocolate fix to warm you up.

TOURISM MID NORTH COAST
W: www.escapenorth.com.au

PACIFIC PALMS HOLIDAYS
209 Boomerang Drive, Bluey's Beach 2428
P: **02 6554 0500** W: www.pacificpalmsholidays.com.au

OR VISIT: **www.visitnsw.com.au**

MURRAY RIVER

The mighty Murray River stretches from the Snowy Mountains to the Southern Ocean. Where to go along its massive length, though, can be overwhelming. I picked South Australia's Riverland district and visited wineries, wetlands and gorgeous country towns and learnt about the river's amazing history.

I dropped into Banrock Station to sample their wines and see their large eco-tourism complex. What used to be a boggy swamp is now flourishing wetlands. The walkways pass over watercourses where all sorts of birds and animals – even Bilbys and Betongs – live. It's wonderfully peaceful and I'm so thankful for what they've achieved.

In Loxton, the 'Garden Town of the Riverland', I had a great chat to Syd Villis, who told me all about the Murray's dark side – flash floods. The Tree of Knowledge, a red river gum near the caravan park, shows various flood levels. 1956 goes down as a memorable year: Syd says the waters were over the ceilings and he floated around town in an old washtub.

The soil here is a farmer's dream, the supply of produce abundant. Stop and buy up big at the famous Berri Direct store. Also pop into Renmark, the oldest settlement on the Murray and home to the beautifully restored paddle steamer, *PS Industry*, for a taste of what life was like in the 1880s.

The ultimate Murray experience, though, has to be a houseboat. My boat was so cool and flash I was steering from the living room! As I drifted along I felt I had the Murray to myself, it was so quiet and well worth every extra mile.

MY TIP

Akuna Station, just outside of Waikerie, is a great place to stay. Throw yourself into farm life, sleep in a restored paddleboat and ask the owners to take you for a meal at the local pub; it's full of characters.

GETTING THERE

Less than two hours' drive north from Adelaide.

WHAT TO DO WHEN IN THE AREA

∞ Great towns in the area to visit: Morgan, Waikerie, Blanchetown, Barmera, Loxton, Berri and Renmark.

∞ Renmark is home to Ruston's Rose Garden, the Paringa Bridge (a suspension bridge that rises daily), the Renmark Hotel and Olive Homestead.

∞ Morgan has the historic ports and museum, a heritage walk, and great organic produce.

∞ The Loxton Historical Village gives you a taste of what life was like back when the area was first settled. If you're there on Village Alive Days, the local folk bring that history alive.

RIVERLAND TOURISM
P: **1300 655 276** W: **www.riverland.info**

WAIKERIE VISITOR INFORMATION CENTRE
Orange Tree Giftmania, Sturt Highway, Waikerie 5330
P: **08 8541 2332** W: **www.waikerietourism.com.au**

BANROCK STATION WINE AND WETLAND CENTRE
Holmes Road, Kingston-On-Murray 5331
P: **08 8583 0299** W: **www.banrockstation.com**

LOXTON RIVER CARAVAN PARK
Riverfront Road, Loxton 5333
P: **08 8584 7862/1800 887 733** W: **www.lrcp.com.au**

BERRI DIRECT SALES
Old Sturt Highway, Berri 5343
P: **08 8582 3321**

AKUNA STATION
Sturt Highway, 25 km east of Waikerie 5330
P: **08 8351 7185** W: **www.akunastation.com.au**

OR VISIT: **www.southaustralia.com**

NEW NORCIA

Could you handle a holiday of absolute silence? Well it's quite something, and well worth the effort to check into the Guesthouse at the New Norcia Monastery. It is Australia's only monastic town and the Benedictine monks here are determined to keep their beloved monastery as is and ensure its survival. They have opened up their blessed doors to the public and 70,000 people drop by to visit or stay every year.

This is serious business as they need around $12 million a year to maintain and preserve the architectural infrastructure. A husband and wife team are now business managers of the town's hotel, roadhouse, art gallery gift shop, farm and world-famous bakery. People come from all over the world to see how the town, monks and tourism operate as one.

Founded by Benedictine monks back in 1846, the site once had an Aboriginal mission and boarding school but is now home to 16 monks seeking prayer and reflection. Feel free to join them in the chapel for their daily prayers. The Guesthouse is reserved for those with serious intentions, who truly want to share the monks lives and devotion. For what it's worth, I failed dismally in my quest for silence while there. Hey, you try phoning home without saying a word. I would have been much better off at the New Norcia Hotel, which is quite lovely, has delicious food and you're free to talk till the cows come home. Praise the Lord for that.

MY TIP

While the bread from the famous New Norcia Bakeries has everyone raving, I recommend the New Norcia Nut Cake – yum! It's baked in the monastery's 100-year-old wood-fired oven, and no doubt blessed with love.

GETTING THERE

Just 133 km northeast of Perth, the town is less than two hours' drive along the Great Northern Highway. A bus also services the town.

WHAT TO DO WHEN IN THE AREA

∞ Check out the history of the town at the monastery archives.

∞ There's a museum and art gallery with artefacts and paintings associated with the monastery. You can pick up the self-guided heritage tour map from both places.

∞ A good way to get your bearings is to join the two-hour guided town walking tour.

NEW NORCIA TOURIST INFORMATION
P: 08 9654 8056

BENEDICTINE COMMUNITY OF NEW NORCIA
Great Northern Highway, New Norcia 6509
P: 08 9654 8018

NEW NORCIA BAKERY
Great Northern Highway, New Norcia 6509
P: 08 9654 8041 W: www.newnorciabaker.com.au

OR VISIT: www.westernaustralia.com

NORTH & SOUTH STRADBROKE

A storm in 1896 cut Straddie in two. Today, North and South are equally successful but vastly different. North is kind of your laidback country cousin, smiling beatifically because they live in paradise. South is your glitzy rello, smirking over their exclusive patch, just a 15-minute jetboat trip to the bright lights of the Gold Coast.

An hour-long vehicular ferry trip gets you to North Straddie and gives you an idea of the mixed bag of holidaymakers you'll be sharing your beaches with. Surfers rave about Main Beach. North Gorge Headland is the best spot for anyone hoping to see the passing migration of humpback whales, but campers will tell you it's from the front of their tents at several foreshore campgrounds. I dare not disagree, but private cottages are popular for families and I loved the Amity Bungalows, where you can fish off a private jetty and snorkel for hours at the nearby beach. Add in great cafes, fish and chip shops, a beer garden at the ol' Stradbroke Island Beach Hotel, ferocious socialising, music that's always cranked up and cheap T-bones – it reminds me of those dreamy, family beach holidays of yesteryear.

South Straddie is an award-winning eco resort – no cars allowed. Most of the island is undeveloped so it's wonderful to explore the lush rainforest, melaleuca wetlands, 22 km of ocean beach and cycle tracks, and to see the odd wallaby and bandicoot. Every accommodation budget is catered for, from camping to nature cabins and private villas at the Couran Cove resort. For a great meal, follow the track to The Surf Club at the resort, where we ate ourselves stupid on seafood, washed down with a nice cold chardie. The island is also a sport-lover's dream with its brilliant facilities – Carl Lewis opened the running track! For families, singles and die-hard romantics, both Straddies are worth the trip.

GETTING THERE

A ferry ride for just you or/and your car departs Cleveland, near the Gold Coast.

WHAT TO DO WHEN IN THE AREA

∞ Lots of tours, including fishing charters, sea kayaking and snorkelling adventures, sandboarding, 4WD treks, camping holidays, golf and bowls days – something for everyone.

∞ Walk the North Gorge past Frenchman's Beach to Point Lookout, a great spot for whale watching.

∞ There's a historical museum in Dunwich on North Straddie, which is well worth checking out.

∞ With all this talk about beaches, don't forget to see the lakes: Brown, a perched lake only a 3.4 km drive from Dunwich; and Keyholes, a system of lakes and lagoons accessible by 4WD off the East Coast Road, among others.

MY TIP

Seafood doesn't get any fresher than on North Straddie as you can buy it direct from fishermen when they get in – signs at Amity Point and Point Lookout direct you to their homes. On South Straddie, those who are romantic at heart should book a dinner at the Mango Chapel.

AMITY BUNGALOWS
33 Ballow Street, Amity Point, North Stradbroke Island 4183
P: 07 5580 3781 W: www.amitybungalows.com.au

STRADBROKE ISLAND BEACH HOTEL
East Coast Rd, Point Lookout, North Stradbroke Island 4183
P: 07 3409 8188 W: www.stradbrokeislandbeachhotel.com.au

COURAN COVE ISLAND RESORT
South Stradbroke Island
P: 07 5597 9000 W: www.couran.com

STRADBROKE ISLAND HOLIDAYS
Shop 2, Raby Bay Harbour, 152 Shore St West, Cleveland 4163
W: www.stradbrokeholidays.com.au

STRADBROKE FERRIES
Toondah Harbour, Middle Street, Cleveland 4163
P: 07 3286 2666 W: www.stradbrokeferries.com.au

OR VISIT: www.queenslandholidays.com.au

PITTWATER & PALM BEACH

Whether you board the 190 bus, a seaplane or limo, pop on over to Pittwater, Sydney's northernmost suburb. The locals loathe the exclusive tag, no doubt earned by the lack of hotels, land space and transport, but the 2108 postcode will never shake that reputation. It's a little unfair, considering how many wonderful experiences there are on this beautiful peninsula – one of them being to stickybeak at the nation's poshest beach houses.

This is a favourite Sydney day trip. People can't get enough of the protected waters, social life and shopping in the area. To explore, start at Barrenjoey Headland, the highest point, which is surrounded by national park. Walk up the Smugglers Track to the lighthouse to see over to the Central Coast, along the Hawkesbury River and down to the sailboat-laden Pittwater and Sydney's Northern Beaches – basically you have calm waters on one side of the peninsula and rolling surf on the other. The lighthouse tour reveals a juicy past. Did you know the customs station was built in 1881 when the waterway was considered the backdoor for Sydney smugglers? Or that the track to the lighthouse was built by convicts? Plenty of interesting characters have lived in the surrounding cottages.

For shopping, head to Bow Wow for year-round beach buys. If you're hungry I have two tips: Barrenjoey Boathouse at the base of the lighthouse – they serve breakfast on the water's edge – and, for over-the-top romantics, Jonah's. The latter opulent institution was built in 1927 when two pounds was all you needed for a block of land! You can catch a seaplane from Rose Bay when you dine there for that extra special evening. But, of course, the water is the true drawcard of this area. I just can't believe this can all be found within an hour of Australia's most manic city.

GETTING THERE

The northernmost suburb of Sydney is just over a 30-minute drive from Sydney's CBD.

Two Inspire offer lots of ways to experience Pittwater, such as kayaking, abseiling and orienteering. It's all about having fun and, as you can guess by their name, motivation.

WHAT TO DO WHEN IN THE AREA

∞ The nearby Newport Arms is a great pub that overlooks Pittwater and all the ritzy and not-so-ritzy yachts that sail the waterway.

∞ The best coffee is to be found at Pronto's Creative Foods, on Barrenjoey Road in Palm Beach.

∞ Star-spotting is big. Many celebs live in the area, and others just visit; oh, and look out for the odd film crew – this area is hot for locations.

BARRENJOEY LIGHTHOUSE
End of Barrenjoey Headland, Palm Beach 2108
W: www.lighthouse.net.au/LIGHTS/NSW/Barrenjoey/
Barrenjoey.htm

BOW WOW
1093 Barrenjoey Road, Palm Beach 2108
P: 02 9974 1762

JONAH'S
69 Bunya Road, Palm Beach 2108
P: 02 9974 5599   W: www.jonahs.com.au

TWO INSPIRE
P: 02 9337 1653   W: www.twoinspire.com

NEWPORT ARMS HOTEL
Cnr Beaconsfield and Kalinya Streets, Newport 2106
P: 02 9997 4900   W: www.newportarms.com.au

OR VISIT: www.visitnsw.com.au

PALM
BEACH
FERRY

SHEFFIELD

Sheffield is the town that turned itself into an art gallery. In 1986, after years of economic decline, the townsfolk were desperate for a way forward. They held a public meeting and one bright spark suggested lining the streets with murals. Sheffield is now so popular they hold a Mural Fest in April each year to unveil new works, when over 120,000 tourists beat a path to its door. The town has earned the title 'Tasmania's Outdoor Gallery'. It's a sight to see.

Sheffield sits on the doorstep of rugged Mount Roland, so the surrounding green rolling hills and lush grazing land meet the edge of this magnificent mountain. One inspiring dairy farmer, Des Brown, took a good look around at his idyllic locale – he has the best views from his property – and decided to share them. He now offers accommodation at his Eagles Nest, and it's not just a place to lay your head but an absolute experience. The lifestyle, the landscape, the luxury – I'd describe this private retreat as hip meets homespun. It has all the mod cons, yet the fittings were built with old classic dairy equipment. Let me explain: the bedheads are made from an old milking machine, and the wonderful table outside is the tractor wheel it looks like. Oh, and you can sample the world's best sofa; it revolves 360 degrees, offering maximun exposure to the views. That Des sure is amazing. Everything about his retreat is inspired; it's kinda quirky and it works. A perfect match for the town of Sheffield.

WHAT TO DO WHEN IN THE AREA

∞ The Kentish Museum displays lots of items relating to the area's past.

∞ Nearby Lake Barrington is great for water sports and walks through this lush area.

∞ One for the young: visit Tasmazia, a large maze complex that will confuse everyone, including Mr and Mrs Crackpot, the owners.

∞ Nearby Kimberly has thermal springs to warm up the proceedings.

MY TIP

Visit Sheffield's general store, Slaters – run by the same family since 1899 – where you'll see the flying fox change dispensing system in full flight, pardon the pun. These were in use long before cash registers were dreamt up.

GETTING THERE

Sheffield is not far from Devon, an hour west of Launceston in Tasmania's north.

EAGLES NEST RETREAT
3 Browns Road, West Kentish, Sheffield 7306
P: 03 6491 1511 W: www.eaglesnestretreat.com.au

TASMAZIA
500 Staverton Road, Promised Land 7306
P: 03 6491 1934 W: www.tasmazia.com.au

SLATERS COUNTRY STORE
52 Main Street, Sheffield 7306
P: 03 6491 112 W: www.slaterscountrystore.com.au

OR VISIT: **www.discovertasmania.com.au**

STRAHAN

This place is all about the landscape. Strahan is the gateway to a World Heritage jewel of temperate rainforest, a precious place we nearly lost to development. I first discovered it while driving from coast to coast. Leaving Mount Darwin I snaked through the Derwent Valley, crawled up the highlands to see the pristine (a common term used here) Lake St Clair and took the route past the Franklin–Gordon Wild Rivers National Park. Finally, I hit the wild West Coast . . . and Strahan.

Much of the area is inaccessible – you just can't drive straight through it. You need to fly over, cruise through, kayak along or walk within to immerse yourself in one of the most isolated outposts on Earth. I certainly felt like I was standing on the edge of the world on Ocean Beach, watching massive waves, propelled by the Roaring Forties, roll in and smash on to the hard shore. For this city girl it was exhilarating.

The sand dunes are stars in their own right, beloved by sandboarding and tobogganing thrill seekers. I should also mention the cool boat trip with Strahan Marine Charters through Hells Gates, the narrow waterway separating the harbour from the Indian Ocean. Just 25 km out to sea you can drop cray pots and fish for mackerel, trout or salmon.

Europeans first came here for the Huon Pine but, me, I'm dazzled by the Gordon River – chilling to think how close it came to being dammed back in the 1980s. Today it stands testament to the environmental movement, a reminder of the need for passionate protection. We should all be proud.

WHAT TO DO WHEN IN THE AREA

∞ See the Gordon River on board a World Heritage Cruises' boat, which are built for comfort and to impact as little as possible on the environment.

∞ A scenic flight will let you see more of the inaccessible parts of the rainforest.

∞ Visit Bonnet Island at the entrance to the Macquarie Harbour; it's home to colonies of penguins and shearwaters.

∞ From Cape Sorell you can look out over the wild Southern Ocean.

∞ Macquarie Restaurant overlooks the harbour and the seafood on offer is straight from the ocean you're looking at.

MY TIP

The Wilderness Railway has been a shot in the arm for local tourism. Train buffs love this steam and diesel trip across 35 bridges, through rainforest and old mining towns.

GETTING THERE

Almost in the middle, but a hop to the west: three hours southwest of Launceston; four hours northwest of Hobart.

STRAHAN MARINE CHARTERS
Low Jetty, Main Wharf, Strahan 7468
P: 03 6471 4300

WEST COAST WILDERNESS RAILWAY
Driffield Street, Queenstown 7467
P: 03 6471 1700

WORLD HERITAGE CRUISES
The Esplanade, Strahan 7468
P: 03 6471 7174   W: www.worldheritagecruises.com.au

MACQUARIE RESTAURANT AND CLIFFTOP LOUNGE
Jolly Street, Strahan 7468
P: 03 6471 7160

OR VISIT: www.discovertasmania.com.au

TAMAR VALLEY

Let's go on a gourmet tour of northern Tasmania. The Tamar River created a rural bonanza: rich vineyards, orchards, pastureland and forests, from Launceston to the sea. The restaurants and cafes here are tops and so are the abundant berries. Pop into Rosevears Estate – they have self-contained apartments I'd love to live in, a restaurant I'd love to always dine at, and wines I'd like to bathe in. Dr Andrew Pirie, arguably one of our greatest winemakers (no doubt you've heard of Ninth Island and Pipers Brook), is based here and these cool climate wines do wonders for the tastebuds.

You will feel like you are stepping back in time at the historic towns south of Launceston. Evandale is the penny-farthing capital of Australia; Woolmers Estate near Longford (see Spring) is home to the best Devonshire tea; Ross is worth seeing just for the bridge covered in 186 Celtic symbols carved by convicts (oh, there's a good bakery too); Tunbridge and Oatlands have extraordinary hawthorn topiary (not for eating, though); and when you make it to Barilla Bay in Meadowbank, order a traveller's pack of oysters. The drive to Deloraine is also gorgeous! At the foot of the Great Western Tiers, you can get into great outdoorsy activites here. Another 100 km on is Burnie. The cheese factory here produces over 20 varieties to add to your thighs, and I loved the lobster man who showed me creatures over a foot long.

There you have it. Easy journeys that are totally different, delivering something for all.

MY TIP

Visit Bicheno, near the Freycinet Peninsula; locals rush here in summer and fishermen love it in the cooler months. If you see Diamond Island, look out for the penguins at dusk.

GETTING THERE

Get to Launceston, hire a car and set off in any direction and prepare for a feast wherever you go.

WHAT TO DO WHEN IN THE AREA

∞ Visit Seahorse World, dine at the Seahorse Cafe Restaurant and look out over the Tamar River.

∞ Don't forget, you're only a boat ride away from King Island here (see Spring), a gourmet paradise!

∞ Stand on the Temptation, Recreation, Salvation and Damnation crossroads in Ross and you'll see the Man-O-Ross Hotel on one corner, the Town Hall on another, a Catholic church on the third and a gaol on the last one. Appropriate, me thinks.

ROSEVEARS ESTATE AND ACCOMODATION
1a Waldhorn Drive, Rosevears 7277
P: **03 6330 1800** W: **www.rosevearsestate.com.au**

EVANDALE VILLAGE FAIR AND
NATIONAL PENNY FARTHING CHAMPIONSHIP
P: **03 6391 8223** W: **www.evandalevillagefair.com**

ROSS VILLAGE BAKERY
15 Church Street, Ross 7209
P: **03 6381 5246** W: **www.rossbakery.com.au**

BARILLA BAY OYSTERS
P: **03 6248 5458** W: **www.barillabay.com.au**

LACTOS CHEESE FACTORY
145 Old Surrey Road, Burnie 7320
P: **03 6433 9255** W: **www.lactos.com.au**

THE SEAHORSE CAFE RESTAURANT
Shed 1A, Inspection Head Wharf,
Flinders Street, Beauty Point 7270
P: **03 6383 4111** W: **www.seahorseworld.com.au**

OR VISIT: **www.discovertasmania.com.au**

TORQUAY TO APOLLO BAY

Are you ready to get wet? Apart from being a great drive, The Great Ocean Road offers some of the most popular surf coast in Australia. So, here's your surfside manual. Torquay is the official start of the road and the unofficial surf capital of the nation. Follow the signs (and the waxheads) down to every surfer's Mecca – Bells Beach. Home to the world's longest-running surf competition in Easter, it was enough for me to just feel the sand between my toes at this sacred site. But, there are at least ten other good surfing options, from Jan Juc to Point Addis. Birdrock is loved by locals but is pretty hardcore; it has a fast, hollow right-hander for the more experienced. Steps is great at low tide, Boobs better at high. You can't beat Winky Pop for consistency, any tide, any swell. Centreside and Southside are both home to a fast right-hander. Jarasite is awesome for tow-ins. Point Addis will get you away from the crowds. Cathedral Rock is only five minutes from Lorne and can claim a world-class right-hander on the lower tide once the swell is four foot and over.

Okay, that sorts the surfers out, but don't worry if that's not you as I've still got a stack of other ideas. Anglesea offers a perfect spot for small children with Point Roadknight, a protected bay. I kinda like it for a sunset stroll. My favourite beach is easy to miss from the road: a tiny one called Petticoat. It's not uncommon to see cute boys diving here for abalone and crays on the nearby reef. Actually, the whole coast is loved by divers and spearfishermen in their crazy camouflage wetties. Nearby, Skenes Creek is also a happy home for families, both human and aquatic.

Do you get the drift? This stretch of coast is not just for driving. It has something for every kind of water baby.

GETTING THERE

From Melbourne, head to Geelong via the West Gate and Princes Highway, about 55 minutes to drive. The Great Ocean Road starts at Geelong and stretches almost all the way to South Australia.

MY TIP

Visit Surfworld Museum to not only learn the history of surfing and see a board being made, but also test your skill by riding a mechanical board.

WHAT TO DO WHEN IN THE AREA

∞ The Great Ocean Road Marathon is in May.

∞ The Otway Fly gets you high up in the canopy of the old growth forest of the Otway Ranges.

∞ At The Heads is now a popular restaurant but was Diver Dan's boatshed in 'Sea Change'.

∞ At Growlers restaurant, say hi to co-owner Nicky Buckley.

∞ The Great Ocean Walk takes you to the edge of the wilds of the Southern Ocean – love it.

GATEWAY TO THE GREAT OCEAN ROAD
W: www.greatoceanrd.org.au

TORQUAY VISITOR CENTRE
Surf City Plaza, Beach Road, Torquay 3228
P: 03 5261 4219 W: www.visitsurfcoast.com

SURFWORLD MUSEUM
Surf City Plaza, Beach Road, Torquay 3228
P: 03 5261 4606 W: www.surfworld.org.au

SURFING TERMS
W: www.surfing-waves.com/surf_talk.htm

OTWAY FLY TREE TOP WALK & CAFE
335 Phillips Track, Beech Forest 3238
P: 03 5235 9200/1800 300 477 W: www.otwayfly.com

AT THE HEADS
Jetty Road, Barwon Heads 3227
P: 03 5254 1277

GROWLERS TORQUAY
23 The Esplanade, Torquay 3228
P: 03 5264 8455

OR VISIT: www.visitvictoria.com

r visiting You Yangs Regional Park

WERRIBEE

You Yang? No, you yang me, I no yang you!

Sorry, but not only is this one of my favourite mountain ranges, I'm incapable of saying its name with a straight face. The memorable title comes from the Aboriginal words *Wurdi Youang* or *Ude Youang*, meaning 'big mountain in the middle of a plain', and that's exactly what Mathew Flinders saw when he scaled the highest point with three other men in 1802.

The Aborigines loved the huge natural hollows in the granite rocks as they held water even in the driest of seasons. I love exploring this place simply because you can come face-to-face with the wildlife while hiking through the massive gums, wattles and sheoaks. I've picnicked at the 'Big Rock' and spent hours looking out over the rich plains below, out to Mount Macedon, the Brisbane Ranges, Geelong and the distant skyscrapers of Melbourne. That's part of the appeal – its proximity to the city.

On your way here you'll pass The Mansion Hotel in Werribee, once the grand home of Scottish immigrants and brothers Thomas and Andrew Chirnside but now one of the state's great tourism success stories. The historic house passed to the Catholic Church, who passed it on to the government, who thankfully tendered it out. The Mansion Group won the bid and they turned it into the five-star boutique hotel. Boy, would those Chirnside brothers love to blow their bagpipes here now.

It's mind-boggling what's been created here. You can pick a rose from the State Rose Garden, take your horse for a giddy-up at the equestrian centre, play a spot of polo and then get that dirt out from under your nails in the day spa. Not to mention sample the wine at Shadowfax, or do your worst on the golf course. Your choice.

You Yang? My word you should.

GETTING THERE

The You Yangs is 55 km southwest of Melbourne, or 22 km north of Geelong. It is clearly signposted via Little River or Lara. The park entrance is on the sealed Turntable Drive.

WHAT TO DO WHEN IN THE AREA

- ∞ Sunday Jazz Session at Shadowfax Winery.
- ∞ Cyclists love this area for the long country roads, canola and wheat flapping in the wind and koalas high up in the trees.
- ∞ Take a tour of the open range zoo, maybe a photographic safari in an open-top jeep through the lower savannah, or take the little nippers on a slumber safari?

MY TIP

To get to the You Yangs, you take the turn off at Little River. Recognise the name? This is where a super-talented young band were around 30-odd years ago, on their way to a gig, when they came up with their band's name . . . the rest, as they say, is history.

YOU YANGS REGIONAL PARK
Turntable Drive, Lara 3212
P: 03 5282 3356/0408 512 580
W: www.parkweb.vic.gov.au/1park_display.cfm

THE MANSION HOTEL
Werribee Park, K Road, Werribee 3030
P: 03 9731 4000 W: www.mansionhotel.com.au

WERRIBEE OPEN RANGE ZOO
K Road, Werribee 3030
P: 03 9731 9600 W: www.zoo.org.au

OR VISIT: **www.visitvictoria.com**

WINTER

ADELAIDE HILLS

I'd be quite happy to spend just a day driving around the lush Adelaide Hills, checking out the magnificent gardens and adjoining mansions, maybe pulling over for a cup of coffee in the town square of Stirling and generally taking it easy. But the truth is, there are too many great B&Bs in the area to treat it as a day trip from Adelaide. My pick is The Orangerie, a romantic French-style villa that makes you feel as though you're holidaying in Provence. The gardens are filled with old European trees, fountains, a pool and court. I love it in winter when it's brisk and cosy inside. But then again, the garden really comes alive in spring, when the bulbs burst with colour. As do the Hills themselves. It's one of those places that is sublime in all seasons.

Try to time your trip to coincide with the Heart of the Hills Market – it's classic country, with amazing local produce to buy. One more suggestion for food (and history) lovers is the town of Hahndorf, Australia's oldest surviving German settlement. They've got the beer, the historic architecture and the bakeries filled with sweety treats. I dare you, though, to sample a spicy sausage from Hahndorf Smallgoods. Manager Don Osbourne uses traditional German recipes and I could barely speak after biting a chilli and cheese kransky. I hate to think what happens to those who go one step further with the Bumburner Mettwurst. The name says it all. Have a cool ale on the ready after this one.

MY TIP

An easy peasy way to check out the best food and vino in this region is a personalised tour. I love 'Life is a Cabernet'; the name alone puts a smile on my face. Ask Ralph to take you to the Salopian Inn in McLaren Vale – so yummy.

GETTING THERE

Travel north by car from Adelaide; it's an easy 20 to 35-minute drive.

WHAT TO DO WHEN IN THE AREA

∞ Sample the wines from South Australia's oldest wine region. There are more than 50 wineries in the Hills, among them Petaluma, Nepenthe, Shaw & Smith, Ashton Hills and Chain of Ponds at Gumeracha.

∞ The Heysen Festival is in September/October and it showcases local arts.

∞ Visit Hans Heysen's house, The Cedars, which is pretty much the same as it was when the artist died in 1969.

∞ Get the best views of Adelaide and Gulf St Vincent from the Mount Lofty Summit.

THE ORANGERIE
4 Orley Avenue, Stirling 5152
P: 08 8339 5458 W: www.orangerie.com.au

HEART OF THE HILLS MARKET
Old Woollen Mill, 1 Adelaide Road, Lobethal 5241
P: 08 8389 5615 W: www.marketsatheart.com

THE FAMOUS HAHNDORF SMALLGOODS
37 Main Street, Hahndorf 5345
P: 08 8268 3845

LIFE IS A CABERNET
P: 0417 807 068 W: www.lifeisacabernet.com.au

SALOPIAN INN
Cnr McMurtrie and Willunga roads, McLaren Vale 5172
P: 08 8323 8769

HEYSEN – THE CEDARS
Heysen Road, Hahndorf 5345
P: 08 8388 7277

OR VISIT: www.southaustralia.com

AYERS ROCK (ULURU)

I couldn't do a book on Aussie locations and not include Ayers Rock . . . it'd be un-Australian, wouldn't it? The image of the Rock is such a potent part of our lives that the first time you spy it you feel something deeply familiar. The sheer scale, the ancient culture (the Anangu people have lived in its shadow for over 30,000 years) and the mysterious stories that have evolved from here, the heart of Australia, will have you rivetted. Our most famous icon truly is magnificent.

My first journey here was with my Nan who, in her eighties, was finally fulfilling a life-long dream. We were equally in awe. Highlights were an excursion to the Olgas, listening to the tales spun by locals who are as fascinating and rich in character as the Rock itself, and the simple joy of circumnavigating the Rock's base. When people talk in hushed tones about the energy, magnetism and spirituality that emanates from it, they're not wrong.

The accommodation is impressive: top marks to Voyages for the variety to choose from. Heaven knows, this place has come a long way since camping in a swag was your only option. Tents are now five-star and you can bed down at Longitude 131°, every bit as fabulous as you may have heard. The luxury, the design, the intimacy and, above all, that staggering view. I slept with my blinds wide open so I didn't miss a single second of the sunrise over the Rock and I can still recall its beauty and gently changing colours. I'm as spellbound now by that memory as I was when I was there.

WHAT TO DO WHEN IN THE AREA

∞ Join Voyages' Desert Awakening 4WD Tour to see the beautiful sunrise over this amazing landscape.

∞ Don't just stick to Uluru – take an excursion further afield to equally grand ancient sites, such as Kings Canyon (see Spring).

∞ Guided walks by the Anangu people take you some of their sacred sites and you learn about the area from a different perspective.

∞ See the Red Centre on the back of a Harley with Patrick from Uluru Motorcycle Tours.

MY TIP

A once in a lifetime experience is the Resort's Sounds of Silence dinner. After watching the sun set over the Olgas and the Rock, dine under a million stars, feasting on all sorts of bush tucker. It does get chilly, though, so rug up.

VOYAGES AYERS ROCK RESORT AND LONGITUDE 131°
Yulara Drive, Yulara 0872
P: 02 8296 8010/1300 134 044 W: www.voyages.com.au

ULURU-KATA TJUTA NATIONAL PARK
P: 08 8956 2299 W: www.ea.gov.au/parks/Uluru

ULURU MOTORCYCLE TOURS
P: 0418 849 707

OR VISIT: www.tourismnt.com.au

GETTING THERE

You can fly directly to and from Alice Springs and Ayers Rock. Once there, join the tours or hire a 4WD to get about.

BLUE MOUNTAINS

Aren't the Blue Mountains the most wonderful saving grace? It is a blessing to such a varied group of wandering souls. We have the adventurer off hiking or canyoning; the romantic fool dining with their lover in a cosy restaurant corner; the health nut working up a sweat in one of the many spa retreats; the green thumbs in their element at Mount Tomah's Botanic Garden or driving the beautiful back roads spying into majestic gardens; the mums and dads in search of an easy escape with child-friendly facilities; the foodie sampling the gourmet treats of the local eateries; the antique lover fossicking for hours in search of a bargain. That covers a lot of bases and I think I fit into nearly all of them! However, I'm just as happy to catch the train from Sydney to escape the city and simply 'take the air', as the Victorians did generations ago.

To be perched atop Echo Point and gazing across the vast Megalong Valley, shrouded in a haze of blue from the oil in the eucalypt leaves, is heaven for me. Or I walk across to The Three Sisters, a path deeply trodden from years of eager tourists. I can also wander for hours through the art deco town of Katoomba or the streets of Leura, checking out their cool shops and cafes. The Paragon is a classic and you'll also find culinary joy at Solitary Restaurant in Leura, Darley's at Lilianfels, and Collits' Inn. Don't worry about the calories – you can mooch it off in a hike through the Mountains' trails.

MY TIP

If you're an adrenaline-seeking sports nut, you'll love the Blue Mountains Adventure Company canyoning tour through ravines carved over millions of years.

GETTING THERE

The Blue Mountains seem to be getting closer all the time as the road improves. It's now just a 90-minute drive from Sydney, or you can catch the train or bus.

WHAT TO DO WHEN IN THE AREA

∞ Scenic World for children of all ages runs the Skyway, Railway, Walkway and Cableway – four great ways of viewing the cliffs from top to bottom.

∞ Lilianfels is one of our best country hotels and it has an amazing spa. Great for a weekend or daytrip.

∞ For that truly special occasion, or when you want to really spoil yourself, try the Sydney Helicopters Blue Mountains Interlude. Unforgettable.

∞ The visitor information and national park offices have a list of 42 walks on offer.

∞ The Jenolan Caves near Oberon are great for a cool underground adventure – literally.

MOUNT TOMAH BOTANIC GARDEN
Bells Line of Road, via Bilpin 2758
P: 02 4567 2154 W: www.rbgsyd.nsw.gov.au

THE PARAGON CAFE
65 Katoomba Street, Katoomba 2780
P: 02 4782 2928

SOLITARY RESTAURANT
90 Cliff Drive, Katoomba 2780
P: 02 4782 1164 W: www.solitary.com.au

LILIANFELS BLUE MOUNTAINS RESORT & SPA
Lilianfels Avenue, Echo Point, Katoomba 2780
P: 02 4780 1200 W: www.lilianfels.com.au

COLLITS' INN
Hartley Vale Road, Hartley Vale 2079
P: 02 6355 2072 W: www.collitsinn.com.au

BLUE MOUNTAINS ADVENTURE COMPANY
84a Bathurst Road, Katoomba 2780
P: 02 4782 1271 W: www.bmac.com.au

SCENIC WORLD
Corner Violet Street and Cliff Road, Katoomba 2780
P: 02 4782 2699 W: www.scenicworld.com.au

SYDNEY HELICOPTERS
25 Wentworth Street, Granville 2142
P: 02 9637 4455 W: www.sydneyhelicopters.com.au

OR VISIT: www.visitnsw.com.au

BOWRAL

There's just something about Bowral in winter, with its roaring fires, vivid colours and historic country feel, that makes me rub my hands together with glee. A wander down the main street, Bong Bong, almost makes me feel like I should be in a Jane Austen novel, which of course I should. Bowral is one of an equally quaint group of Southern Highland towns like Mittagong, Berrima, Bundanoon and Moss Vale; all beloved by the horsey set, who no doubt cherish the feeling they've found a little patch of the motherland so close to Sydney.

The colours of this region are always a wonder. Bowral enjoys true seasons, hence the exquisite gardens, but I love it when it's chilly and you can just escape to this region for a weekend of cosying up in wonderful restaurants, or playing board games, or toasting marshmallows on one of the many roaring fires. For those of us not blessed with a country manor house, you can still feel 'to the manor born' when you stay at either Milton Park owned by Anthony Hordern of department store fame in the 1900s – or the slightly more affordable Briars Lodge, famous for its steaks. Both grand old buildings have sprawling gardens. You can also fly fish at Briars and sample the day spa at Milton.

A good day out in Bowral would be a visit to Mount Gibraltar, the Bradman Museum or the Bong Bong racecourse. Markets are also huge, with one on just about every weekend. There's a lot to do in this area. Whether you escape the city for the day or you give it a week, you'll get a wonderful country hit, be beautifully looked after and feel gloriously comfy at any time of year.

MY TIP

I love a fair or market. Every second Saturday the Bowral Farmers Market hits town. This is a food lover's paradise.

GETTING THERE

Bowral is a 75-minute drive southwest of Sydney.

WHAT TO DO WHEN IN THE AREA

- ∞ The thing to do in any Southern Highlands town is to shop. The Mittagong Antiques Centre is a fave.
- ∞ The area is famous for its cool climate wines; Centennial Vineyard or Southern Highlands Wines offer a top cellar door service.
- ∞ Bushwalking and horse riding are wonderful because of the lovely surroundings.
- ∞ The Bowral golf course will keep the golfers happy.
- ∞ For pampering try Glam, the most beautiful perfumery with a day spa out the back.

MILTON PARK COUNTRY HOUSE HOTEL
Hordens Road, Bowral 2576
P: 02 4861 1522   W: www.milton-park.com.au

BRIARS LODGE AND INN
653 Moss Vale Road, Bowral 2576
P: 02 4868 3566   W: www.briars.com.au

BRADMAN MUSEUM
St Jude Street, Bowral 2576
P: 02 4862 1247   W: www.bradman.org.au

BONG BONG PICNIC RACE CLUB
Kangaloon Road, East Bowral 2576
P: 02 4861 4494   W: www.bongbongprc.com.au

MITTAGONG ANTIQUES CENTRE
84–7 Main Street, Mittagong 2575
P: 02 4872 3198

CENTENNIAL VINEYARDS
Woodside, Centennial Road, Bowral 2576
P: 02 4861 8700

SOUTHERN HIGHLANDS WINES
Cnr Olbury Road and Illawarra Highway, Sutton Forest 2577
P: 02 4868 2300   W: www.southernhighlandwines.com

BOWRAL COUNTRY CLUB
Cnr Centennial Road and Boronia Street, Bowral 2576
P: 02 4861 1946   W: www.bowralcountryclub.com.au

GLAM FRAGRANCE AND BEAUTY
325 Bong Bong Street, Bowral 2576
P: 02 4862 2660

OR VISIT: WWW.VISITNSW.COM.AU

BROKEN HILL

Lights, camera, action! Broken Hill has hit the big time – think Hollywood meets the outback. Many people associate this region with its extraordinary mining history but it's also brimming with creativity and inspiration. Loads of movies have been shot here – *Mad Max*; *A Town Like Alice*; *Priscilla, Queen of the Desert*; *Mission Impossible 2* – as well as music clips, commercials and TV shows. Perhaps this is because of the long, uninterrupted vistas, the light and colours of the landscape, the friendly nature of the locals; this town is happy to accommodate big crews as well as us wee travellers.

Pro Hart is a fine example of how the colours of the area inspire. His work is proudly displayed throughout the town; it even greets you at the airport – love that mural! Jack Absolom and Eric Minchin and loads of new artists keep the tradition alive. To let your own imagination loose, head out to Living Desert Reserve for wonderful landscapes to paint or photograph. The Sculpture Symposium has displayed amazing works here, created by a group of artists in 1993. Go at sunset with a bottle of champers and watch the light filter through Bajo El Sol Jaguar (Under the Jaguar Sun).

The region is perfectly summed up for me by the Regional Art Gallery. Great works of Australian art were donated by BHP to the miners, and the collection is valued at over $10 million, possibly the most altruistic action by a mining company. The area may be considered 'outback', but clearly it has an energy that inspires all.

MY TIP

Definitely have a drink at Mario's Palace, the crazy hotel where Priscilla was shot. Only the murals painted by an Aboriginal gentleman, Gordon Way, have been added since it was first built.

GETTING THERE

Broken Hill is 1,165 km west of Sydney; 48 km east of the SA border. It has an airport, and trains and buses stop there.

WHAT TO DO WHEN IN THE AREA

∞ Seek out a blooming Sturt Desert Pea, named after the explorer who came to the region in 1844 searching for the inland sea. His diary noted the discovery of a 'broken hill'.

∞ For more movie magic, visit Silverton, 25 km away. It's nearly a ghost town these days, but film producers can't get enough of its classic character. The original pub is a great place for a beer and bite, and to hear the goss on Mel Gibson, apparently lovely but tiny.

∞ Check out Albert Woodroffe's Horizon Gallery in Silverton.

∞ The Imperial in Broken Hill is run by the same people who do most of the catering for film crews.

PRO HART GALLERY
108 Wyman Street, Broken Hill 2880
P: 08 8087 2441 W: www.prohart.com.au

BROKEN HILL SCULPTURE SYMPOSIUM
The Living Desert Reserve, 9 kms from Broken Hill
P: 08 8080 2289 W: www.brokenhill.nsw.gov.au

BROKEN HILL REGIONAL ART GALLERY
404–8 Argent Street, Broken Hill 2880
P: 08 8088 6897
W: www.artgallery.brokenhill.nsw.gov.au

MARIOS PALACE HOTEL
Argent Street, Broken Hill 2880
P: 08 8088 1699

SILVERTON HOTEL
Layard Street, Silverton 2880
P: 08 8088 5313

THE HORIZON GALLERY
Cnr Burke and Layard Street, Silverton 2880
P: 08 8088 5331

THE IMPERIAL FINE ACCOMMODATION
88 Oxide Street, Broken Hill 2880
P: 08 8087 7444
W: www.imperialfineaccommodation.com

OR VISIT: www.visitnsw.com.au

BROOME

I love Broome in winter. There's nothing finer than pressing your pasty white body on to the creamy white sands of Cable Beach, letting that gorgeous sun tickle your shoulders. Keep clear of the camels that lollop up and down carrying giggling tourists, though. Also, make sure you sign up for a Broome Windrider Safari, a combination of kayak, trimaran and windsurfer that'll whizz you along the coast, heading north to explore deserted, prisitine beaches.

My first visit to Broome was pure serendipity. I just never knew the west was so darn gorgeous during the east's chilliest months. The beaches are lined with tanned backpackers and travellers of all ages. Broome is ultra laidback and very relaxed around unusual characters, possibly because it owes its success to such people – a blend of colonial Australian, Japanese, Chinese and Aboriginal cultures. That mix is reflected in the food (Matso's is fantastic), the art (artists sell their works on the streets) and the shopping (don't even think about going home without a pearl).

Broome is the 'Port of Pearls', so why not stay at McAlpine House, once the home of a pearling master, then the man who put Broome on the tourist map, Lord McAlpine. Today, we can thank Marilyn Paspaley for its slick refurbishment. Set in a quiet part of town, away from the crowds and hidden behind palms, it is incredibly close to the beach. They throw a weekly cocktail party, serving champagne and 'pearl meat' (yummy oysters) soaked in citrus and lemongrass. Sublime.

WHAT TO DO WHEN IN THE AREA

∞ Paddle across the turquoise waters checking out the red sandstone fossils and finish with a hermit crab race on a secluded beach.

∞ Sun Pictures is the world's oldest outdoor operating picture garden. You have to go.

∞ Visit Gantheaume Point at low tide to see dinosaur footprints, about 130 million years old.

∞ True to its heritage, Broome has a thriving Chinatown.

BROOME VISITOR CENTRE
Cnr Broome Hwy and Bagot Street, Broome 6725
P: 08 9192 2222/1800 883 777
W: www.broomevisitorcentre.com.au

WINDRIDER SAFARIS
P: 0407 010 772

MATSO'S BROOME BREWERY
60 Hamersley Street, Broome 6725
P: 08 9193 5811 W: www.matsosbroomebrewery.com.au

MCALPINE HOUSE
84 Herbert Street, Broome 6725
P: 08 9192 3886 W: www.mcalpinehouse.com

WESTERN BLUE SEA KAYAK
Cable Beach, Broome 6725
P: 1300 665 888 W: www.westernblue.com.au

SUN PICTURES
27 Carnarvon Street, Broome 6725
P: 08 9192 1077 W: www.sunpictures.com.au

OR VISIT: www.westernaustralia.com

MY TIP

From April to November the Western Blue Sea Kayak guys offer many trips out exploring the coastline in their kayaks. Turtle Bay at sunset is tops.

GETTING THERE

About 2,200 km north of Perth along the Great Northern Highway, you can drive, fly, bus or sail to Broome.

BYRON HINTERLAND

With all respect, sometimes the best thing about Byron is leaving it, turning your back on those glorious beaches and heading up into the hills to explore the many country towns dotted throughout the hinterland. Once you cross the highway, life really slows down and there are still many working farms up here, so expect to stop the car to let cattle cross the road. It's lush and peaceful, with hippies, farming families and a quieter type of tourist, all mixing in together.

I always seem to get lost on these back roads but sometimes that leads to wonderful discoveries, like Newrybar near Bangalow. I was making my way to interview Olivia Newton-John at her retreat when I found the most wonderful little group of shops. The Harvest Cafe is fantastic and I picked up some really cool pressies in the antique stores. Thankfully, I did make it to Gaia, a retreat dedicated to restoring, refreshing and renewing your mind, body and soul. Extra care is taken here and you can choose to do everything or nothing, and most of the food is grown in their vegie garden and orchard. I just loved the place.

There's something about the whole of the hinterland that inspires creativity. In Bangalow and Mullumbimby you'll find shops with unique designs, gifts, great live music and cool cafes. The Crystal Castle near Mullumbimby, where you can have your aura read, is so tranquil you wander through in a virtual daze. So, just hop in the car, drive and be loose with your plans. This truly is a peaceful region to explore.

MY TIP

The Green Mango has gone from strength to strength since I first visited. Ask to stay in The Bails, a self-contained cottage with a view of the valley that'll make you sigh.

GETTING THERE

The hinterland towns are within easy drive of Byron Bay, 790 km north of Sydney, 180 km south of Brisbane.

WHAT TO DO WHEN IN THE AREA

∞ At Mullumbimby I had the best roast ever at the Middle Pub and chilled out at Poinciana Cafe.

∞ Federal is almost a one-store town, but check out Pogel's Wood. Mmmm.

∞ Bangalow is the jewel of the area and one of my favourite shopping strips in Australia.

∞ Mooball is home to the Moo Moo Cafe: if you can eat two Moo burgers at once, the second is free.

∞ At Coorabell is the wonderful Coorabella Guesthouse, an old Queenslander transported here by designer Giovanni D'Ercole.

HARVEST CAFE
18 Old Pacific Highway, Newrybar 2479
P: 02 6687 2544 W: www.harvestcafe.com.au

GAIA RETREAT & SPA
933 Fernleigh Road, Brooklet 2479
P: 02 6687 1216 W: www.gaiaretreat.com.au

CRYSTAL CASTLE
Monet Drive, Montecollum 2482
P: 02 6684 3111 W: www.crystalcastle.net

GREEN MANGO HIDEAWAY
Lofts Road, Coorabell 2479
P: 02 6684 7171 W: www.greenmango.com.au

THE MIDDLE PUB
46 Burringbar Street, Mullumbimby 2482
P: 02 6684 3229

POINCIANA CAFE
55 Station st, Mullumbimby 2482
P: 02 6684 4036

POGELS WOOD CAFE & RESTAURANT
Lot 1 Federal Drive, Federal 2480
P: 02 6688 4121

MOO MOO CAFE
Ampol, Pacific Highway, Mooball 2483
P: 02 6677 1230

COORABELLA
895 Coolamon Scenic Drive, Coorabell 2479
P: 02 6684 6610

OR VISIT: www.visitnsw.com.au

CAIRNS

Cairns has had a facelift and she doesn't care who knows about it. With its perfect location between rainforest and reef, it was, shall we say, something of a visual disappointment for tourists. What greets you today, though, is a dazzling multimillion-dollar spruce up that is genuinely exciting. Instead of mudflats you'll find an amphitheatre, picnic areas, walking tracks, shops and unbelievable restaurants.

Cairns will always be the kick-off point to other adventures: for tropical islands and reef, head east; for the Atherton Tablelands, go west; for World Heritage national parks, travel north; and for rugged ranges, waterfalls and lakes, head south. But, the base city is now great to return to, again and again. During my last stay, I started each day with a dip in the saltwater swimming lagoon, so big it can fit up to 1,000 bobbing bods. Often I'd join in on an aquarobics class with the locals – cool fun and no stingers!

The Wildlife Dome, atop the casino, has an amazing display of wildlife, rainforest flora and fauna. I loved the virtual face-to-face contact you can have with a saltwater croc; thrilling. Another absolute 'must visit' is The Regional Gallery, where you'll find works from local, Cape York and Torres Strait artists. The indigenous jewellery I bought at KickArts is admired by people all over the world.

This town has finally evolved into the star its location demands and it appears the facelift has created a proud international city. Go girl!

MY TIP

Starting life as a small show in Kuranda (first train stop up to the Tableland), the Tjapukai Aboriginal Cultural Park is truly a success story for the local indigenous people.

GETTING THERE

Cairns is the 'capital' of Far North Queensland and has an international airport, as well as good road and rail access.

WHAT TO DO WHEN IN THE AREA

∞ The brilliant Tropic Days is a world-class backpackers right in the heart of town.

∞ Stroll along the Cairns Esplanade; it's dog and people friendly.

∞ I loved the Ken Done Gallery in Cairns. It spans two floors and the massive artworks are mesmerising.

∞ Passionate foodies are spoilt for choice. My all-time fave meal was at The Red Ochre – who knew roo and croc could taste so good?

∞ The Esplanade comes alive at night with buskers and dancers, the heat seems to draw everyone to the streets.

SWIMMING LAGOON
Cairns Esplanade, Cairns 4870

THE REEF HOTEL CASINO
35–41 Wharf Street, Cairns 4870
P: 07 4030 8888 W: www.reefcasino.com.au

CAIRNS REGIONAL GALLERY
Cnr Abbott and Shields streets, Cairns 4870
P: 07 4046 4800 W: www.cairnsregionalgallery.com.au

KICKARTS
98 Abbott Street, Cairns 4870
P: 07 4050 9494 W: www.kickarts.org.au

TJAPUKAI ABORIGINAL CULTURAL PARK
Kamerunga Road, Smithfield 4878
P: 07 4042 9900 W: www.tjapukai.com.au

TROPIC DAYS BACKPACKERS
26–28 Bunting Street, Cairns 4870
P: 07 4041 1521 W: www.tropicdays.com.au

KEN DONE GALLERY
4 Spence Street, Cairns 4870
P: 07 4031 5592 W: www.done.com.au

RED OCHRE GRILL
43 Shields Street, Cairns 4870
P: 07 4051 0100 W: www.redochregrill.com.au

OR VISIT: www.queenslandholidays.com.au

DAINTREE

'Where the rainforest meets the sea' is apt. Cape Tribulation is the only place on the planet where you'll find two World Heritage-listed environments cosying up to each other: the Great Barrier Reef and the Daintree Rainforest. The drive up from Cairns will get you in the mood as one after another of jaw-droppingly beautiful sights reveal themselves. Then, when you find yourself immersed in the Daintree, prepare to be mesmerised. This is basically the world's oldest living museum – we're talking about 110 million years of primeval beauty. I've visited many times and can't wait to return.

My favourite spots include Mossman Gorge, where the waters are crystal clear and ice cold; Cow Bay and Thornton Beach, which are beautiful to explore and you might just see a dugong in the waters; and the Discovery Centre which is tops. The Dubuji visitors' area has free barbies, a rainforest boardwalk and a track to Myall Beach. My most memorable day trip was cruising the croc-infested waters of the Daintree River – just keep your little fingers inside the boat here.

Where you stay is of little consequence as everyone shares the same lush paradise and the choice is good. Silky Oaks and Thala Beach Lodge are high-end. Coconut Beach Rainforest Resort has a great position. The nightlife for backpackers is fantastic at PK's Jungle Village. When it comes to writing your 'things I must do before I cark it' list, there is no question the Daintree must be on it.

MY TIP

If you see a bottle of vinegar at a beach entrance, don't use it for your fish and chips. It's a cure-all for wounds inflicted by stingers in the water.

GETTING THERE

From Cairns, head north past Port Douglas. Hiring a car is a popular option, as are heliport transfers that land on various properties.

WHAT TO DO WHEN IN THE AREA

∞ Join a croc tour and find out the safe spots to swim in the area.

∞ There are plenty of hiking trails to get you up close and personal with the rainforest, but if a cassowary crosses your path, give it right of way – they have been known to kill.

∞ Chill out on the beaches; they are exquisite.

∞ Join a boating trip out to the reef.

DAINTREE DISCOVERY CENTRE
Corner Cape Tribulation Rd and Tulip Oak Rd, Cow Bay 4873
P: 07 4098 917 W: www.daintree-rec.com.au

VOYAGES SILKY OAKS LODGE
Finlayville Road, Mossman 4873
P: 1300 134 044 W: www.silkyoakslodge.com.au

THALA BEACH LODGE
Private Road, Oak Beach, Port Douglas 4871
P: 07 4098 5700 W: www.thala.com

COCONUT BEACH RAINFOREST RESORT
Cape Tribulation Road, Cape Tribulation 4873
P: 07 4098 0033/1800 816 525

PK'S JUNGLE VILLAGE BACKPACKERS
Cape Tribution Road, Cape Tribulation 2873
P: 07 4098 0040 W: www.pksjunglevillage.com.au

DAINTREE ECOLODGE
20 Daintree Road, Daintree 4873
W: www.daintree-ecolodge.com.au

COCKATOO HILL RETREAT
13 Cape Tribulation Road, Daintree 4873
P: 07 4098 9277 W: www.cockatoohillretreat.com.au

OR VISIT: www.queenslandholidays.com.au

DARWIN

Darwin is where optimism runs as freely as the beer. It's a buzzing, multicultural, wild, artistic hub and, boy, do these locals know how to have a good time. Cyclone Tracy may have devastated Darwin back in 1974, but it was down, not out. With bravado, it has re-bloomed, full of energy. It's also packed with characters from all over the world as people come here to reinvent themselves. I understand the appeal: work in shorts, reasonable real estate prices and a laidback lifestlye. As one taxi driver put it to me, 'Darwin's got "future" written all over it and I'm on board for the duration!'

In winter, we southerners head north for fun in the sun as the dry season kicks in (summer is the wet season, when you'll get awesome lightning displays). I also love the Mindil Beach Sunset Markets. The smile never leaves my dial as I wander from store to store collecting food to eat on the beach as the sun does its final dance for the day. My mum and I were lucky enough to be at Paspaley's head office when a shipment of their world-famous pearls came in off the boat. They let us dunk our hands into the full buckets and we savoured every second. If Darwin is your kick-off point to maybe Kakadu or Lichfield Park, stock up at the General Store, which has been in business for more than 25 years. Their motto: 'You can't go bush without seeing us first'.

Darwin is so raw and has a style all of its own, kinda like the locals. I'm always planning my next visit. I suppose I'm with the cabbie: I'm definitely on board for the duration.

WHAT TO DO WHEN IN THE AREA

∞ Take a boat trip to the Tiwi Islands, only 80 km from Darwin.

∞ Visit Fannie Bay Gaol, built in 1883. You'll find the gallows on display and a Cyclone Tracy exhibit.

∞ The Darwin Festival kicks off in August. It is a distinctly multicultural event.

MINDIL BEACH SUNSET MARKETS
Mindil Beach, Darwin 0800
P: 08 8981 3454 W: www.darcity.nt.gov.au

PASPALEY PEARLS
Paspaley Pearl Building, Smith St, Darwin 0800
P: 08 8982 5555 W: www.paspaleypearls.com

NT GENERAL STORE
42 Cavenagh Street, Darwin 0800
P: 08 8981 8242

ADELAIDE RIVER QUEEN CRUISES
Adelaide River Bridge, Arnhem Hwy, Via Humpty Doo 0821
P: 08 8898 8144 W: www.jumpingcrocodilecruises.com.au

FANNIE BAY GAOL MUSEUM
East Point Road, Darwin 0800
P: 08 8999 8290

DARWIN FESTIVAL
P: 08 8981 0083 W: www.darwinfestival.org.au

OR VISIT: www.tourismnt.com.au

MY TIP

To this day, one of the best tours I've done is the Jumping Croc Tour with Adelaide River Queen – any closer to the crocs and I wouldn't be around to tell the story.

GETTING THERE

Darwin is the captial of the Northern Territory and lies on the north coast. It is well serviced by air, road and rail.

ELSEY CREEK STATION

The book, *We of The Never Never*, by Jeannie Gunn is the story of one woman's adventures on a cattle station comprising millions of acres of Aboriginal land. Disected by the Roper River, the land is now back in the hands of its original inhabitants, the Mangarrayi people. They allow only one operator, Mike Keighley, to take guests through their home. To turn your holdiay into the trip of a lifetime, you need a guide respected by the locals, and that's Mike.

This is not a tour, but rather an experience of a land that seems to have stood still. I was amazed at how the Mangarrayi have learned to make the most of the environment and trust the seasons. I looked at a kapok tree and saw pretty yellow flowers, but the children knew that it meant turtles had laid their eggs, ready to be collected for food. While we swam in the river, the kids dived under and came up with the promised bounty. Mike also took us further up river as crocs slid in one by one and barramundi virtually jumped into our boat. The next day we swam in a thermal pool, surrounded by paperbarks and palms. I was scared at first but Mike reassured me and I'm grateful he pushed me out of my comfort zone.

That night, as dinner was being prepared over the campfire, I slipped back into the bush jacuzzi, glass of champers in hand, and stared up at the star canopy. I knew I was experiencing something rare and extraordinary. Jeannie Gunn wrote in 1905 about 'A land so intoxicating that if you live in it and love it you'll never never want to leave it'. A hundred years later it's still enchanting.

MY TIP

You'll double the joy of your holiday if you speak to as many of the locals as possible.

GETTING THERE

The Katherine region is not too difficult to travel to as it's just 324 km south of Darwin.

WHAT TO DO WHEN IN THE AREA

∞ To immerse yourself in equally surreal environments and meet the true locals, join one of Mike's other tours. You'll never, never regret it.

∞ An equally great company to tour with is Gecko, who canoe through Katherine Gorge and stop at places named Dead Man's Drop and Boat Cruncher.

∞ This area is filled with bird-life, enough to turn you into an ornithologist.

MIKE KEIGHLEY, FAR OUT ADVENTURES
PO Box 54, Katherine 0851
P: 0427 152 288 W: www.farout.com.au

GECKO TOURS
PO Box 304, Katherine 0851
P: 1800 634 319 W: www.geckocanoeing.com.au

OR VISIT: www.tourismnt.com.au

FARAWAY BAY

After so many years of travelling for a living, I'm sure some people think I must have been everywhere. The joy of travel, though, is that it's infinite. There are always new places to discover, to dream about and to wish for. Right now, I'm starry-eyed about the remote Faraway Bay in the Kimberley, the outback of the outback. I've only just discovered that this far-flung paradise exists, and now I yearn for its remoteness and its unique wilderness experience.

People talk about the daunting challenge of accessing this area, but just getting there is part of the appeal for me. To leave the city behind and dive into a pre-historic world, with soaring sandstone cliffs, cascading waterfalls, tidal rivers, sprawling mangroves, sunbaking crocs and dense rainforest teeming with wildlife. What an adventure.

Faraway Bay is perched on a tiny headland, in the northwest corner of our vast continent. They call it a Bush Camp, but this coastal hideaway in the middle of nowhere sounds like the ultimate in rustic luxury. The bungalows apparently disappear into the landscape yet have 180-degree water views, along with a stone bordered pool and an open-air dining room that serves luscious, healthy meals. All this makes me feel weak at the knees with desire to be there and be part of this dream location – apparently it just can't be beaten.

The owner studied the coastline by chopper, all 350 km of it, to pick the perfect spot. When I get there, and I will, I want to spend my days bushwalking the whole surrounding area, discovering the many Aboriginal rock galleries hidden in the cliffs, or just flaking out under the warm sun during wintertime. Sounds dreamy, sounds good – think I'm going to have to turn this one into a reality.

GETTING THERE

The only ways in are via the air or sea. Small light aircrafts from Kununurra take you to a private airstrip, then you'll travel via 4WD to The Bush Camp. Or you can charter a boat and make your way up the coast.

WHAT TO DO WHEN IN THE AREA

∞ While in the Kimberley, why not extend that flight in or out and travel over the Bungle Bungles?

∞ Just simply revel in the fact that you can explore an area that is basically uncharted.

∞ 'Dinghy taxis' are on offer, so you can find your own deserted beach, and they'll pack a picnic lunch for you.

MY TIP

The Orion (see Summer) travels past here on one of her trips, so maybe that's another good way in.

THE BUSH CAMP
Faraway Bay, Kimberley
W: www.farawaybay.com.au

OR VISIT: www.westernaustralia.com

HOTHAM

Hotham is hot! When it comes to Aussie ski fields, this is the one with the best buzz, for all sorts of reasons. Easy access: it's the only snow resort with its own airport. On the field: Hotham sits high on the mountain, so you can drive there, park your car and ski to and from your accommodation. Accommodation sorted: all budgets covered – Absollut is worth popping your head into just to squiz at the luxury. Après-skiers sorted: day spas and shopping galore, Zirky's being a crowd fave. Snowboarders sorted: a fantastic terrain for this booming sport. Kids sorted: they have a separate area from the main runs, so they're always safe. No pretences: Hotham is a little grungier and less showy than other resorts. But to be honest, I love it because it's a true skier's mountain: quality powder snow, long and varied runs, smack dab in the middle of the beautiful Victorian Alps.

Now about the nightlife. You may like to know that bars on the mountain are open till 2 a.m. and free buses ferry you home till 3 a.m., and that's brilliant. Swindlers, showcasing Melbourne's best bands and DJs, is continuously voted best alpine bar. The White Room might be black on the inside but the mood is never dull. It surely has the grooviest cocktail bar and the yummiest food. Groovers sorted.

Snow resorts are notoriously competitive, wafting in and out of fashion. I can't keep up with all the latest offerings but I do register consistency. It's a credit to Hotham that it keeps itself fresh and its market continuously happy. As I said, Hotham is hot, even when it's cold outside.

MY TIP

On a sunny day, few things could be finer than stopping off at Snake Gully Hut. Have your hot chocky on the balcony and watch life literally whoosh by.

GETTING THERE

Mount Hotham is in the Victorian ski fields, about a four-hour drive northeast of Melbourne. The airport is 20 km away.

WHAT TO DO WHEN IN THE AREA

∞ With the airport right there, why stay? Feel free to fly in and fly out in a day.

∞ Dinner Plain is a great village not too far from the action and accommodation is often cheaper.

∞ Onsen is a Japanese-inspired complex at Dinner Plain, complete with restaurants, a pool, day spa, salon and a brilliant restaurant, Tsubo, for sushi-lovers like me.

∞ Horse riding is available during summer, as are other great alpine sports.

MOUNT HOTHAM ALPINE RESORT
Great Alpine Road, Mt Hotham 3741
P: 03 5759 3550 W: www.mthotham.com.au

ABSOLLUT APARTMENTS
Great Alpine Road, Mt Hotham 3741
P: 03 5759 3550

ZIRKY'S
Great Alpine Road, Mt Hotham 3741
P: 1800 3545 55 W: www.zirkys.com.au

SWINDLERS BAR & RESTAURANT
Great Alpine Road, Mt Hotham 3741
P: 03 5759 4421

THE WHITE ROOM
Great Alpine Road, Mt Hotham 3741
P: 03 5759 3456

DINNER PLAIN CENTRAL RESERVATIONS
PO Box 48, Dinner Plain 3898
P: 1800 670 019 W: www.dinnerplain.com

OR VISIT: www.visitvictoria.com

LINDEMAN ISLAND

Okay, little ones, this is for you. You'll love me for this one and I'll even throw in a few tricks to get your parents here.

This island has a distinct village feel. People of all ages return year after year because they feel as though they're part of a family. Lindeman is a member of Club Med, the first resort company to master the all-inclusive package holiday. Club Med also invented Kids Club, now copied in resorts everywhere. For you, that means full-on activities. On this island your parents don't need to carry money, either – they have a currency book. So there's no need to worry about tipping or change since everything is pre-paid. It's that simple. No one will get cabin fever, either, as there's heaps to do, with rainforest walks, day spas, two pools, two bars, a nightclub, and entertainment every night. But did I mention the circus school? My childhood dreams of running away with one came true here. I was able to try my luck on the trapeze, ten metres off the ground with only a net between me and certain death! I was truly awful at it. If you're good, though, you'll get extra classes, a lycra suit and the chance to be in a sunset show for everyone on the island. I wish that had been me.

When I went to Lindeman I kinda expected the worst. Would this be 'Melrose Place' on sand? I can't deny I ended up having a ball on this classic gorgeous isle overlooking the Whitsunday Passage. Lindeman offer an experience that is now mimicked on other islands, it's that good. Even if you're a goose on the trapeze like me, fun is guaranteed.

WHAT TO DO WHEN IN THE AREA

∞ With seven beaches, have a go at snorkelling and oystering.

∞ Butterfly Valley is a wonderful place for a stroll.

∞ Climb Mount Oldfield (212 metres) to see Pentecost, Hamilton and other Whitsunday islands.

∞ You can easily power a dinghy to the nearby little islands for a bit of an escape.

MY TIP

During school holidays the island runs Kidz World Packages, which feature selected performers, sporting events and eco adventures.

GETTING THERE

The nearest airport is on Hamilton Island, or you can catch a boat from Shute Harbour, near Airlie Beach.

CLUB MED
Lindeman Island, Whitsundays
P: 02 9265 0500/1300 855 052 W: www.clubmed.com.au
OR VISIT: www.queenslandholidays.com.au

LIZARD ISLAND

You'll be besotted by Lizard Island, the most northern of the Reef's resorts. It's renowned for its privacy, exclusivity and natural beauty. The local Dingaal Aborigines say this group of islands looks like a stingray, with Lizard being the head and the others forming the body. I did spot plenty of rays during my stay, which was filled with . . . alarming moments.

Firstly, the island's namesake – how are you with lizards? Big ones at that. We're talking metre-long, languid, licking whoppers – the Gould's sand monitor to be precise. To be fair, they mean no harm and they were here first. I was just a tad startled by them, but not half as alarmed as the morning I went swimming and discovered massive fish right alongside me. These harmless but copious creatures are what they say makes Lizard so special, along with the gardens of underwater coral, turtles and brightly coloured fish just a few freestyle strokes from the shore. The resort keeps guest numbers to a minimum so you can always find a quiet spot for yourself. Or you can hire a tinny and head off to find your own beach. When I did this I got stuck on the reef and a tiny shark turned up. Arghh! I was rescued by a near-naked man, who was having a quiet moment with his beloved on their honeymoon!

I don't mean to scare you. This island is sublime and relaxed enough to poke fun at itself; the resort is completely OTT and I highly recommend a brief sojourn. But do be careful in those impossibly beautiful waters . . . you never know what lies beneath!

MY TIP

Get yourself out to the Cod Hole, where you can dive down in the impossibly clear water and sit at the bottom of the ocean, watching giant cods hover overhead.

GETTING THERE

Flights to Lizard Island are via Cairns.

WHAT TO DO WHEN IN THE AREA

- ∞ Catamarans, paddle skis and glass-bottom boats will get you out to the deeper reef.
- ∞ Learn to dive, snorkel or play tennis.
- ∞ The island has wonderful walking trails.
- ∞ Take a trip to the Research Station and watch the work of the tropical scientists.
- ∞ Dine at Osprey's, where the food is out of this world and the mood relaxed.

VOYAGES LIZARD ISLAND RESORT
P: 02 8296 8010/1300 134 044 W: www.lizardisland.com.au
OR VISIT: www.queenslandholidays.com.au

MELBOURNE

Nobody does sport like Melbourne – it's their religion, passion and heartbeat. Best of all, they love to share it, whatever the sport, with whoever's keen to turn up. From our first Olympic Games to the latest and most successful Commonwealth Games, Melbourne does it with ease.

Sports buffs revel in having so many stadiums so close to the city. Summer is Grand Slam tennis at the Rod Laver Arena. Autumn is the world's most legendary surf carnival at Bells Beach, while hoons hoof it over to Albert Park for the Grand Prix. Spring sees Flemington proudly host the race that stops a nation, the Melbourne Cup. But nothing grips Melbourne like AFL, which started here way back in 1896.

Winter is officially footy season. In this town it's nothing short of tribal. When a Melburnian guy asks you out his opening question will probably be, 'So which team do you barrack for?' If you don't know the rules I strongly suggest a great night out with Melbourne Sports Tours, who'll take you behind the scenes of the city's great venues. You'll gain a whole new appreciation for this sport's crazy state. Ask Anthony and Kirsty any silly questions like, 'Who is Mark?', 'Could the shorts be any tighter?', 'Why does everyone hate Collingwood?' while you chomp into a meat pie. It's so much fun, I'd join them even if you do know the rules.

Melburnians would bet on cockroaches crawling up the wall if they could, it's all sport to them and it's always more than a game.

WHAT TO DO WHEN IN THE AREA

∞ Melbourne Sports Tours will even take you up to Mount Buller for a Snow Tour and Bells Beach for the Surf Coast Tour.

∞ For those not so sports-minded (are they any of you left out there?) see Spring and Autumn for more great Melbourne moments.

AUSTRALIAN OPEN TENNIS GRAND SLAM
Rod Laver Arena, Batman Avenue, Melbourne 3000
P: 03 9914 4400 W: www.australianopen.com.au

AUSTRALIAN FORMULA 1 GRAND PRIX
220 Albert Road, South Melbourne 3205
P: 03 9258 7100 W: cars.grandprix.com.au

VICTORIAN RACING CLUB
448 Epsom Road, Flemington 3031
P: 1300 727 575 W: www.vrc.net.au

AUSTRALIAN FOOTBALL LEAGUE
W: afl.com.au

MELBOURNE SPORTS TOURS
P: 03 8802 4547 W: www.melbournesportstours.com.au

OR VISIT: www.visitvictoria.com

TIP

Everyone is obsessed with footy tipping. On Thursday night you put your bid in and the 16 teams battle it out at the weekend. On Monday you either celebrate or commiserate.

GETTING THERE

All roads lead to Melbourne, eventually, as do planes, trains and buses. Just get there and join in the fun.

NINGALOO

If there's one thing I've noticed about veteran TV travel reporters, we all have a sense of adventure . . . and good teeth. It helps to be fearless and, although I might scream like a girl, I'm up for anything. Shark dives are very popular at the moment. My favourite such dive was among the great whites at Port Lincoln with Calypso, but for some strange reason not everyone likes the 'Greats'. So how would you feel about whale sharks in the beautiful waters of Ningaloo? C'mon, even my wimpiest friends could handle this. They're really just the world's biggest fish species, 12 metres long and 11 tonnes of polka dot beauty. Trust me, they're cute!

Why Ningaloo? Well, it's Australia's largest fringe reef and the only one in the world so close to a continental landmass. You can basically walk off the shore and on to the reef. Here, there are 500 species of fish and 200 species of coral. Cue the whale sharks. Once a year, during the coral spawn, when millions of bright pink egg and sperm bundles are released simultaneously, it's a whale shark's buffet. They're not interested in your fleshy bottom; they love the plankton. You're almost guaranteed a spotting. Exmouth Diving flies a plane ahead to detect a location, then you're motored out to the spot, and in you plop. You must be a capable swimmer as you have to snorkel, and you can't touch the sharks. But these creatures do come right to the surface and sometimes right up to you. This is a surreal, intimate, once in a lifetime wildlife encounter. I won't bug you about swimming with great whites if you promise me you'll have a go at this one.

WHAT TO DO WHEN IN THE AREA

∞ Ningaloo Marine Park stretches from Coral Bay, around the North West Cape to Exmouth. So there's plenty to explore on land and sea.

∞ During winter humpback whales migrate through, so start spotting.

∞ Stay at the Ningaloo Lighthouse Caravan Park, which has views to the lighthouse and over the beach.

∞ Diving is huge here, so have a go.

MY TIP

Divers love the Navy Pier, where the fish are abundant. Even the reclusive frog fish is known to make an appearance.

GETTING THERE

Exmouth is 1,270 km from Perth. Coral Bay marks the southern extreme of the reef.

CALYPSO STAR CHARTER
5 Willowbridge Grove, Burnside 5066
P: 08 8364 4428 W: www.calypsostarcharter.com.au

EXMOUTH DIVING CENTRE
Payne Street, Exmouth 6707
P: 08 9949 1201 W: www.exmouthdiving.com.au

LIGHTHOUSE CARAVAN PARK
Yardie Creek Road, Vlamingh Head, Exmouth 6707
P: 08 9949 1478 W: www.ningaloolighthouse.com

OR VISIT: www.westernaustralia.com

NOOSA

You just try holding this old warhorse down! My goodness, Noosa has seen its fair share of booms and busts, from having its famous main beach washed away, to developers running riot. But nothing can alter the beauty of the Noosa National Park or the town's glorious laidback feel.

This holiday spot has something for everyone all year round. My sister loves to take her family here in the warmer months to swim all week – it's safe and easy. Other friends plough through the list of world-class restaurants – Seasons, Berardo's and Sails. Shoppers are also in heaven on Hastings Street, where you'll find bookstores, homeware outlets, designer label boutiques and cafes. I like to combine the lot, especially in winter when it's not as packed. I wander through the National Park in the morning, spotting koalas, and then check out the surf as it never seems to be too cold to take a dip. On Saturdays I head off to Eumundi Markets (see Summer) but the nights are always spent at the yummy restaurants. Then I wake up and do it all over again.

Renting a house or unit is the thing to do with families and groups of friends. Book early as this place is popular. I love Palmyra, nestled within its own rainforest with to-die-for interiors, an infinity pool and even a resident family of kangaroos. Work trips rarely have me lounging around for long as there is so much to film around here, but personal trips always have me returning to just relax and take it easy under the warm winter sun.

MY TIP

For the romantic at heart, take a gondala tour with Ricardo (Richard to his friends), who will glide you along the river as you nibble from a seafood platter and sip on champers.

GETTING THERE

Noosa is just a two-hour drive north of Brisbane, along the Bruce Highway.

WHAT TO DO WHEN IN THE AREA

∞ In June the Noosa Long Weekend gets underway. Conceived by local playwright David Williamson and a group of culture lovers, it's a celebration of drama, literature, film, music, visual arts, food and wine, the environment and the community. Not to be missed.

∞ Canoe through the stunning Everglades, just a 30-minute drive from Noosa.

∞ Kite-boarding and motorgliding are two interesting ways to get around.

∞ On the way to Eumundi, look out for a funky cafe called Alfresco. Great for brekkie and lunch, and flipping through mags dating back to the 1930s.

TOURISM NOOSA
Hastings Street, Noosa Heads 4567
P: 1300 066 672 W: www.tourismnoosa.com.au

SEASONS
5/25 Hastings Street, Noosa Heads 4567
P: 07 5447 3747

BERARDO'S RESTAURANT AND BAR
On the beach, Hastings Street, Noosa Heads 4567
P: 07 5448 0888

SAILS
Hastings Street, Noosa Heads 4567
P: 07 5447 4235

PALMYRA
15 mins from Noosa, in Hinterland
P: 03 9419 9433

NOOSA LONGWEEKEND
P: 07 5474 9941 W: www.noosalongweekend.com

ALFRESCO CAFE
777 Noosa–Eumundi Road, Noosa Valley 4562
P: 1800 667 767

OR VISIT: www.queenslandholidays.com.au

PHILLIP ISLAND

Whenever I think of this magical island, images of families and beaches, motorcycle races and merry penguins spring to mind. Okay, the penguins spring in first, but what's funny is that while these cuties bring in droves of tourists, the locals pay little attention to them. My friends there think the beaches are far better than a parade of waddlers, although one local dad said they used to love it as a romantic date spot. They tried to convince the girls to stay out late by saying it was far better to watch the penguins go out at dawn rather than come in at dusk. Cheeky devils! These days, a grandstand is packed with spectators from all over the world, all straining to see the 30-cm penguins. But don't forget, the island is also home to Australia's largest colony of seals, about 16,000 of them. You can see them and other marine life at Nobbies.

Phillip Islanders live just two hours from the city but they always seem to be in holiday mode, wearing that telling look of, 'Yeah, we know we've got it good'. The island is divided into little towns, each with its own character. Rhyll (my sentimental fave) is quaint and fishing oriented, Woolamai is beloved by surfies and Nobbies is great for diving. Boating is big everywhere and the fishing is first class. Uncle Bill at Phillip Island Marina will set you up nicely and I recommend Western Port Bay to drop a line.

I know the locals would love to keep Phillip Island to themselves – they're only human but with its combination of surf, fishing and wildlife, its the ultimate weekender.

MY TIP

Vino, anyone? There's a buzz around the cool climate wines from this island, so try and sample some at Purple Hen Wines, Bass River Winery and Phillip Island Vineyard.

GETTING THERE

An easy drive one and a half hour drive from Melbourne along the South Gippsland Highway.

WHAT TO DO WHEN IN THE AREA

∞ Just as the island shrugs off winter the motorbikes start roaring in the Australian Motorcycle Grand Prix in September.

∞ The boardwalk at the Koala Conservation Centre (managed by the Nature Park) provides top views of these national icons in their natural habitat.

PHILLIP ISLAND NATURE PARK
PO Box 97, Cowes 3922
P: 03 5951 2800 W: www.penguins.org.au

PHILLIP ISLAND MARINA
P: 03 5956 9238

PHILLIP ISLAND MOTORCYLE GRAND PRIX
W: www.bikes.grandprix.com.au

COMMUNITY GUIDE TO PHILLIP ISLAND
W: www.phillipisland.net.au

PURPLE HEN WINES
96 McFees Road, Rhyll 3923
P: 03 5956 9244 W: www.purplehenwines.com.au

BASS RIVER WINERY
20 St Helier Road, The Gurdies 3984
P: 03 6531 5997

PHILLIP ISLAND VINEYARD & WINERY
PO Box 635, Cowes 3922
P: 03 5956 8465 W: www.phillipislandwines.com

OR VISIT: www.visitvictoria.com

ROBE

It's the howling sou'-westers – wild winds from the Antarctic – that you'll remember of this historic coastal town at this time of year. Tourist numbers drop from around 15,000 in summer to 1,500 in winter as the population moves inland to warmer climes. The locals seem to roll with these highs and lows and this is a great place to escape the maddening crowd, and to experience rollicking weather – just how some of us like it.

Robe is in Guichen Bay. At the height of the tourist invasion there's a thriving beach culture here and seafood and wine seemingly on tap. I sampled the area for the first time just as the crayfish season was winding down and fell in love with its juicy history, salty characters and ripper seafood. At the harvest's peak the boats pull in over 300 crays a day. You can dine on them for brekkie, lunch and dinner. Brian Lawrie and his three brothers, third-generation fishermen, took me out to sea one morning on their boat, appropriately called *No Fear*, to remove live catch from the pots. I had the time of my life. They told me stories of when life was simpler in Robe – now, with crays selling for $60 a kilo, the town has grown somewhat, but it's historic charms remain.

I can totally understand why Rayna Fahey, a former east coast gal, visited Robe just once and fell in love with it. She upped sticks and moved here, converting fishermen's homes into stylish seaside cottages that you'll want to live in all the time. Apart from running Lifestyle Properties, Rayna also has the coolest homewares store in town. Like Robe, her sunny spirit and style blows those winds away.

WHAT TO DO WHEN IN THE AREA

- ∞ Check out the town's original buildings like Robe Hotel, Robe House and Customs House.

- ∞ The dunes are great for 4WD adventures, or you can walk the 12 km of Long Beach.

- ∞ There's a fantastic menu on offer at the Caledonian Inn.

- ∞ The nearby town of Beachport is brilliant for fishing in its aquamarine waters.

ROBE VISITOR INFORMATION CENTRE
Robe Library, Mundy Terrace, Robe 5276
P: 08 8768 2465 W: www.robe.sa.gov.au

BRIAN LAWRIE
Cheyenne Fishing Charters, Robe 5276
P: 08 8767 2985/0428 672 985

LIFESTYLE PROPERTIES
P: 08 8768 5044 W: www.robe.sa.gov.au/robelifestyle/

CALEDONIAN INN
1 Victoria Street, Robe 5276
P: 08 8768 2029

OR VISIT: www.southaustralia.com

MY TIP

The best crays can be found at Starke's Oceana Seafood at the wharf. Kate wraps them up perfectly, lemons and all.

GETTING THERE

Robe is on the Limestone Coast between Adelaide (340 km away) and Melbourne (580 km).

SYDNEY

It's loud, it's rude, it's fast, it's crude! Yes, I've heard the complaints about my home town a thousand times over, but when the sun is shining in winter (nearly all the time), it just makes you sigh with joy to live here. Please let me show you a quiet side of Sydney that keeps us homegrown here forever.

I fell in love with my city all over again when I signed up for a guided kayak tour of the harbour. To experience one of the world's most famous waterways under your own steam is entirely different to a ferry excursion – although I highly recommend that, too. We went under the Harbour Bridge, waved to the Governor General at Admiralty House (actually I think it was a security guard) and had a front row peek into the expensive real estate at Lavender Bay, all with a bit of commentary thrown in. Then there are the harbour foreshore walks. I like the one in Mosman that takes you from Chowder Bay to Taronga Zoo, but I also rate a wander from Manly to Spit Bridge. The Bondi to Bronte walk is the best one to do for people watching. The Harbour Circle Walk is also garnering rave reviews; it's a remarkable effort run by volunteers and loops 26 kms from the Bridge to Hunters Hill.

Finally, may I recommend a day trip to one of our treasure islands? We have at least eight in the harbour open to the public, with Shark, Fort Dennison, Clark and Cockatoo the most popular. Sydney is so much more than Darling Harbour and Bondi. It often gets a bad rap (jealousy's a curse) but no one can deny its natural beauty and spunky spark.

MY TIP

Balmoral is my favourite winter beach. You can go sailing or take a harbour view bush walk, and then dine at one of Sydney's top restaurants, The Bathers Pavilion. It's heaven!

GETTING THERE

The best way to arrive is to fly in over the harbour. Just look out the window in awe.

WHAT TO DO WHEN IN THE AREA

∞ The Manly ferry takes you from the Heads to the Quay, the best-valued trip on the harbour.

∞ Will and Toby's Manly Beach is great any time of day.

∞ Gunners' Barracks is perfect for afternoon tea. It was closed to the public for over 100 years now we can't get enough of it.

∞ The Glenmore Hotel has one of the best city skyline views.

NATURAL WANDERS
Lavender Bay Wharf, Lavender Bay 2060
P: 02 9899 1001 W: www.kayaksydney.com

MANLY KAYAKS
Oceanworld, West Esplanade, Manly 2095
P: 0411 247 917 W: www.manlykayaks.com.au

SYDNEY HARBOUR FERRIES
P: 02 9207 3170 W: www.sydneyferries.info

CITY OF SYDNEY HISTORIC WALKING TOUR GUIDES
W: www.cityofsydney.nsw.gov.au/AboutSydney/
VisitorGuidesInformation/HistoricalWalkingTours.asp

NSW GOVERNMENT – WALKING SYDNEY HARBOUR
W: www.planning.nsw.gov.au/harbour/walking.asp

SYDNEY HARBOUR NATIONAL PARK
W: www.nationalparks.nsw.gov.au/npws.nsf/content/Shark+
Clark+and+Rodd+Islands+Sydney+Harbour

GLENMORE HOTEL
96 Cumberland Street, The Rocks 2000
P: 02 9247 4794 W: www.glenmorehotel.com.au

GUNNERS' BARRACKS
End of Suakin Drive (off Middle Head Road),
Georges Heights 2088
P: 02 8962 5900 W: www.thetearoom.com.au

BATHERS' PAVILION
4 The Esplanade, Balmoral Beach 2088
P: 02 9969 5050 W: www.batherspavilion.com.au

WILL AND TOBY'S MANLY BEACH
8–13 South Steyne, Manly 2095
P: 02 9977 5944 W: www.willandtobys.com.au

OR VISIT: www.visitnsw.com.au

WELLINGTON

I could not have greeted Wellington on a finer day – it was raining and in this rural community that's gold! When a crusty old farmer rolled down the middle of main street atop his vintage tractor and gently waved at me, I knew I was going to like this place. Yes, Wellington is another gorgeous country town, where the locals are satisfied by the simple things in life and, I must admit, it is a little bit like stepping back to the 1950s. However, where they once made their way with sheep and grain, tourism is now kicking in with the dollars. Let's face it, we'd all like a slice of that country joy.

Take the Hermitage Hill, where I stayed. Its former life, for 85 years, was as the district hospital. Now it's designated a National Trust property and has been lovingly restored. The new managers constantly hear stories, from both old hospital staff and patients, of the nurses' cheeky antics in what's now the guest house. If only the walls could talk. I stayed in a beautiful old stone cottage with a spa bath. I dare you to sleep in the Old Morgue, which must be haunted. The Main Ward dates back to 1903 and is home to the town's most popular restaurant, Red Rosellas. It was packed the day I went there and I personally recommend the steak – they leave the fat on.

Need a family excursion? We had a ball at the Angora Farm, where Virginia and Lyle Wykes have a mini zoo. Surely one of the strangest sights I've ever seen was an Angora rabbit being shorn. I guess they have to get the fur somehow; I just wasn't expecting the rabbit to be tied down and tickled with shears. We were even treated to a fashion parade of sorts at the end to show us the process of washing the yarn, treating it with eucalyptus oil, then spinning it.

This is why we love our country holidays. They're a reality check for us city slickers who question whether joy can be found walking through life at a relaxed pace. Yes, it can.

GETTING THERE

Wellington is the second-oldest town west of the Blue Mountains and is located at the junction of the Macquarie and Bell rivers, 370 km north-west of Sydney.

MY TIP

The Visitors Centre has great publications about the local attractions, including 'Historic Wellington', all the info you need on Wellington Caves, Lake Burrendong, Stuart Town and Mount Arthur Reserve, and a well-produced pamphlet about farmstay accommodation.

WHAT TO DO WHEN IN THE AREA

∞ Take a historic walk and see the Commerical Hotel (dated 1865), St Patrick's Catholic Church (1914) and the Convent of Mercy (1896).

∞ The Oxley Historical Museum in a very elegant two-storey brick building erected in 1883.

∞ Lake Burrendong is a huge lake, three and a half times the size of Sydney Harbour, built between 1946 and 1967 to irrigate farmland.

WELLINGTON VISITORS CENTRE
Cameron Park, Nanima Crescent, Wellington 2820
P: 02 6845 1733/1800 621 614

HERMITAGE HILL COUNTRY RESORT
135 Maxwell Street, Wellington 2820
P: 02 6845 4469 W: www.hermitagehill.com

WELLINGTON ANGORA FARM
Gamboola, Yeoval 2868
P: 02 6846 4039

OR VISIT: www.visitnsw.com.au

WROTHAM PARK

There's a clear trend evolving within our tourism market and it's known as the 'Authentic Outback Experience'. Travellers, particularly overseas visitors, don't want to check into a big hotel and be isolated from the locals any more. They want the amazing 'experience'; to meet true blue characters and enjoy unique destinations in every sense of the words. Wrotham Park Lodge is such a location.

Wrotham has been a booming cattle station since the gold rush days of the 1800s. Its almost 600,000 hectares in size. To get your head around that, we're talking two-thirds the size of the ACT; bigger than the Grand Canyon. It has over 35,000 heads of gorgeous Brahman cattle, which are mustered twice a year, around April and September. The musters take about two months, so get your boots on and muck in.

Guests love being thrown into station life. Unlike the stockmen, though, they don't sleep in swags but in king-size beds in 'quarters' that would make R.M. Williams proud. Just get a load of the showers. A massive shower rose pummels you with rainwater as you look out of a floor-to-ceiling window on to the remote rugged wilderness. Breathtaking.

You'll have earned a decent feed after your day on the land and the food has an upmarket Aussie twist. What you're experiencing at Wrotham is the real thing – nothing's fake. Just ask Ol' Tony, who's been mustering here for 30 years, as his Dad did before him. He's happy to chat and guests are delighted to listen. This is pure Aussie outback stuff, hard yakka, with a lil' bit of five-star to soften the edges. Yee hah!

MY TIP

At night when it gets chilly settle in beside the 44-gallon drum fire on the deck and enjoy champers and canapes.

GETTING THERE

About 300 km west of Cairns. Charter flight and helicopters fly in to Wrotham, or you can self-drive.

WHAT TO DO WHEN IN THE AREA

∞ Horse riding, as you can imagine, is big here.

∞ Chopper rides are far and away the most fun thing to do. The chopper is normally used for the cattle muster but the nifty pilot is happy to whip you around anywhere – an amazing experience.

∞ Winter star gazing can't be beaten. The nearest town is hundreds of kilometres away so the sky is clear as; it seems to go on forever.

VOYAGES WROTHAM PARK LODGE
P: 02 8296 8010 W: www.wrothampark.com.au

OR VISIT: www.queenslandholidays.com.au

A-Z LOCATIONS